How Christians Worship

How Christians Worship

The Foundation Series
Volume Four

by

Kenneth N. Myers

Majeux Press
SHERMAN, TEXAS

How Christians Worship
The Foundation Series, Volume Four

© Copyright 2010 by Kenneth N. Myers

Unless otherwise indicated, Scripture is taken from the
HOLY BIBLE, NEW INTERNATIONAL VERSION.
Copyright 1973, 1978, 1984 International Bible Society
Used by permission of Zondervan Bible Publishers.

Scripture quotations marked ESV are from the Holy Bible,
English Standard Version, copyright 2001 by Crossway
Bibles, a division of Good News Publishers. Used by
permission. All rights reserved.

Myers, Kenneth Neal, 1959-
How Christians Worship/Kenneth N. Myers

ISBN 1453677119
LCCN 2010909920

1. Worship   2. Theology   3. Sacraments   4. Liturgy

248

Cover design: Neal Mayeux
Photograph: *El Mesquita, Cordoba Spain* by Neal Mayeux

Published by Mayeux Press
P.O. Box 3497, Sherman, TX 75091

To The Ladies In My Life

My mother Mary
My wife Shirley
My daughter Stormie
My daughters-in-law Megan and Sarah

To the elect lady -
Christ Church Cathedral

and to my favorite niece.

Acknowledgements

Thank you to Robert Webber, who has joined that great company in heaven, whose books started me on my journey of worship, and who was my friend.

Thank you to Scott Rudy, Kenneth Myers II and Chris Goldsmith for proofreading, suggestions and insights.

Table of Contents

Preface to the Series

Too many Christians don't know what it really means to be Christian. Some think that "being good" is what it is all about. Some think that holding a general idea about Jesus - that he died for our sins and rose again from the dead - encompasses all that is needed. Too many, in the modern culture, choose to define for themselves the core definitions of the faith: "well, *for me* being a Christian means..." Others say, "Oh, it's all such a bother. I'll just let the clergy worry about that, and I'll go to church and worship God and live my life."

I would suggest (mimicking here the ancient teachings of the Church) that there are four basic considerations Christians need in order to be fully rounded and secure in their faith.

Belief

What you believe matters. As others have pointed out before me, if you believe five and five makes ten, and you make a five dollar purchase and give the cashier a ten dollar bill, you will not be satisfied with two dollars in change. Belief matters in the real world. It defines us, and it defines our relationships with others - including our relationship with God. Obviously, belief is not just a religious or spiritual matter. Belief affects every aspect of life. If you believe too much sun can cause skin cancer, you will stay out of too much sun. If you believe all Cretans are liars, you won't trust what a Cretan says to you. In the same way, what you believe about God, Jesus, the Church, salvation and the afterlife has an impact on your everyday living, and on your expectations of the future.

Actions

Actions speak louder than words. Everyone has heard this axiom. The Christian faith is not simply a set of theological statements, it also entails how we *act* in our lives. Certainly this flows from our beliefs - real beliefs are played out in what we *do*. Too often people who consider themselves

Christian do none of the things that follow true belief.

Saint James wrote, "Show me your faith without deeds, and I will show you my faith by what I *do*...You see that a person is justified by what he *does* and not by faith alone" (James 2.18,24). Just because you say it doesn't necessarily make it so. Actions matter.

Spirituality

Some people hear the word "spirituality" and think of some kind of mystical spookiness, some kind of otherworldiness that causes super-holy others to walk around as if on a cloud. But *everyone* possesses some form of spirituality. By spirituality I mean how we relate to God in a genuine personal relationship and how it impacts our relationship with ourselves and with others. The chief means of cultivating a Christian spirituality is through prayer, and yet many believers either do not pray at all, or else pray very haltingly, not really knowing *how* to pray.

When we read about godly men and women of the past, we realize they were all people of prayer, including Jesus, who, though he was God come in the flesh, made it his habit to spend quality time in prayer and to teach others how to do the same.

Worship

Finally, Christians who are well-rounded in their faith are people who worship God, and they worship God together with other believers. Far from being a coincidental aspect of true faith, worshipping God with the Church is core to what it means to be Christian. The writer of Hebrews admonished his readers, "Let us not give up meeting together, as some are in the habit of doing, but let us encourage one another - and all the more as you see the Day approaching" (Hebrews 10.25). Just as in the case of prayer, many Christians have no idea *how* to worship. Worship may be seen by some as simply singing a few songs and listening to a sermon. Others insist they don't need to gather with God's people and worship because they can worship God alone out in nature. Still others consider themselves too holy to stoop to gathering with lesser beings and simply stay at home and "do their own thing," while yet others do nothing at all. None of these folk realize that the Bible has much to say about the "what" and the "how" of worship.

A Fourfold Plan

I propose four volumes outlining the Christian faith in popular, easy to understand fashion.

Volume One deals with what Christians believe, and focuses on the ancient Creeds of the Church which capsulize true belief.

Volume Two deals with how Christians behave and focuses on the ethics given by God to Moses in the Ten Commandments.

Volume Three deals with how Christians pray and focuses on the model Jesus gave his disciples in response to their request that he teach them to pray - the Lord's Prayer or the Our Father.

Volume Four deals with how Christians worship and focuses on the two aspects of biblical worship: Word and Sacraments.

It should be said that these books are written first and primarily from a Christian perspective which believes the Bible to be the authoritative Word of God and believes that God has moved in his Church and directed it throughout history. It is also written from an Anglican perspective, a viewpoint that sees itself as "Catholic" (that is, rooted in the ancient, undivided faith) and "Protestant" (that is, calling for a continual reformation of the people of God, having the Holy Scriptures as an unerring guide to all matters of belief, action, spirituality and worship. The Anglican faith in one sense finds its roots all the way back with the Apostles, and in another sense finds its roots in the ancient Celtic/British/English church - the church of St. Patrick, St. Columba, St. Hilda, and more recently influential Christians like C.S. Lewis, J.I. Packer and a host of others.

If the words of these books have a decidedly Anglican focus, the things to which they speak are much more broad in scope and possess a truth that can be shared by all Christians. My prayer is that these volumes will be used as instruments to enrich all Christians who study them, whatever their denomination or tradition.

Finally, anyone addressing the topics before us - from what Christians believe to how Christians worship - finds himself confronted with an inexhaustible amount of data. Literally millions of sermons on these subjects have been preached over the course of the last 2000 years. Thousands of books have been written about them. The goal of this series is not to be exhaustive, nor even to say everything that is important about the subjects at hand, but to provide a popular level of understanding, thoroughly rooted in Scripture. These books are intentionally designed to be used in personal reading, Sunday School classes and small group studies. You will notice that the chapters are chock-full of Scriptures. Please do not give in to the temptation to skip over the Scripture texts, thinking you already know what they say. Let them speak to you in a new and fresh way. While I recognize that I can't say everything worthy of being said, I do truly hope that what is written here will stir up minds and hearts and cause people to dig deeper into other resources. I have appended a suggested reading list at the end. What we have before us when we deal with these noble subjects is treasure. It is worth digging for.

Introduction

The Play's The Thing

The church in which I grew up believed that going to movies was a sin. The first movie I went to came to town when I was about fourteen, and it was a documentary about Bigfoot. It wasn't a real movie - it was a documentary which happened to be screened at the local main street walk-in - some Bigfoot hunter was there too, answering questions afterwards. But getting permission to attend that show was a herculean feat of convincing my folk that this wasn't like "going to the movies," and they only reluctantly allowed me to go.

The first *real* movie I saw was in 1977, on my honeymoon, which happened to coincide with the release of the first *Star Wars* movie. My wife and I drove 60 miles to Dallas, bought our tickets, and ducked inside hoping no one from church saw us, because although we were convinced there was nothing wrong with attending the theater, most of our church folk hadn't yet come to this conclusion. This was heart pounding, breathtaking, edge of your seat stuff - and I'm not talking about the movie, I'm talking about the adventure of getting into the movie without being seen!

By the time I had children, movies had become acceptable in our circles with everyone enjoying them except the most recalcitrant old timers, and by the time I had grandchildren I had made up for the loss of my youth with a passion. Which leads me to this: have you ever been to a movie where, at the end of the show, the crowd just goes crazy and breaks out with applause and whistles of approval? It doesn't happen often, but I've seen it occur a time or two. It happened to me once when I went to see the movie *Luther*, and coincidentally attended with a large group of Midwesterners from the local Lutheran church. As Luther preached the gospel on the big screen, they were shouting and applauding louder and more vehemently than they ever would on Sunday morning in their own services.

Some people think going to church is kind of like going to a movie. All the people in the congregation are the audience. The pastor, musicians and singers are the actors, and the service is the show. We are here to be entertained. If the church across town offers a better show, maybe that's where we'll go next week. Sometimes churches like this have weekly leadership meetings to discuss how the show went, how the audience responded to various elements, how it can be tweaked and improved, and what "bigger" thing can be introduced to draw an even bigger audience in the future.

Worship *is* a drama. But beyond this, the analogy has been applied in a way that is completely wrong. Backwards, in fact.

Worship Is A Drama

Before you read the next paragraph, take a moment and in your own mind list the elements necessary to produce a great Broadway play. We'll just leave the rest of this page blank so you won't be tempted to cheat and read ahead.

What did you come up with? Here is my list:

Audience
Cast and Crew
Director
Stage
The Acts (a one act play? two? three?)
The Script
Costumes and Props
The Climax

I would suggest that these very things are what goes into our Sunday worship of God. Let's unpack the imagery a bit.

The Audience

I once asked a group of pastors how many people each of them had in the audience every Sunday. The responses were varied - fifty, close to a hundred, several hundred - but all the answers were wrong, and they all betrayed a mistaken notion that has crept into the Church in modern times. There is only one person in the audience, God himself. Everyone else has a part to play.

In other words, what we do on the Lord's Day is not for us, it is for God. About the only aspect of this ancient understanding that has survived in many churches today is the word *service*. Signs posted in front of churches say, "Worship Service: 10 A.M." Worship *service*; the service of worship; the service we provide God in our act of worship. We are the servants and God is the one served.

The worship service, then, is best seen as a drama, but not just any kind of drama. It is a command performance. It is a drama performed at the request of the King. God has commanded us to worship him, and throughout Scripture he has instructed us to do this worship not only personally and in our daily living, but also corporately, as a great drama of thanksgiving to him, offered with joy for his many blessings and mercies bestowed on us. This principle is bedrock to biblical faith. When Jesus was tempted by Satan to fall at his feet and worship him, he responded by quoting Deuteronomy 6.13 and said, "*Worship* the Lord your God and *serve* him only" (Luke 4.8).

The Cast And Crew

If God is the only one in the audience, then everyone else involved in the worship service is part of the cast and crew. We are the actors who come before the King to offer great thanksgiving to him. Too many folk think of the "actors" as the "people up front" - the pastor or priest, the musicians and singers, the readers and preachers, etc. We have even gotten into the bad habit of referring to the worship area as *the auditorium* (auditorium - from *audio* - a place to go and listen). But again, this is a wrongheaded focus. We gather as the Church of the Living God to offer him praise through the great drama of worship, and every believer in the gathering has an important action - an important *act*, an important *role* - to perform. The "stage" isn't the elevated front part of the church, the stage is the whole place, where the people are (and by extension, as Shakespeare said, "All the world's a stage"). We need to flip the diagram in our minds: the stage is where the people are doing the acting! In the historic church, the elevated, front part of the church, with the altar as central, is seen as the throne room of God (and while I'm at it, we need to recover the historic language of the Church regarding the building: narthex, nave and sanctuary, but that's another discussion for another time and place).

In Chapters One through Three we will explore this great cast of characters, the Church. We will learn the Church's nature, historic qualities and purpose.

The Director

Every good play needs a good director to oversee the production. In the Church, God has established a three-fold structure of leadership: bishops, priests (if this word bothers you, you can say "elders" - for now) and deacons. But again, we must understand: these men are not the ones "doing the work" - they are called by God to teach, equip, and direct the marvelous cast members in their worship. Saint Paul wrote that Christ, "gave some to be apostles, some to be prophets, some to be evangelists, and some to be pastors and teachers, to prepare God's people for *works of service...*" (Ephesians 4.11-12).

In Chapter Four we will give our attention to the Apostolic Ministry that God has set in place to lead the Church.

The Script

What would a play be without a script? Chaos, that's what! Some churches have put such a premium on spontaneity that they have completely lost the sense of godly order. While the liturgy itself is part of the script, the primary text which the Church uses to worship God (not only corporately on Sunday, but in every act of worship in our daily lives) is Holy Scripture, the Bible, the Word of God. The Bible must be central in our worship of God. It must be read, preached, and lived. It must guide everything else that we do in worship and in life.

In Chapters Five through Seven we will explore the Bible, where we got it, and how to use it.

The Acts

Obviously, a play has acts. Well, a play has at least one act. The drama of worship has four acts, and each act is integral to the overall performance which we offer to the Lord. Briefly put, these acts are:

> The Entrance
> The Service of the Word
> The Service of the Table
> The Dismissal

Each act of the drama is important and adds to the flow of the whole service. In Chapters Eight and Nine we will look at the ancient liturgy of the Church, rooted in the Old Testament, shaped by the Apostles, and handed down through the centuries to this very day.

The Score

Some dramas are musicals - whether they are Renaissance Italian operas or modern Andrew Lloyd-Webber productions, music is core to the show. From the time of the Apostles, Christians have incorporated music and singing as an important element in worship. Chapter Ten will explore the place of music in our drama of thanksgiving.

Showtime

As actors know, timing is everything. An untimely line can ruin everything. Time is important in our worship of God too. Christ has redeemed time for his glory. In Chapter Eleven we will explore the use of time in our worship of God as we look at the rhythms of the week and the Church Year.

Characters, Costumes, And Props

I have attended plays on Broadway with elaborate stages, costumes and props. I have also attended children's Christmas plays with nothing more for costumes than old bath robes. But the accoutrements can make or break a production. Not many directors can pull off a play where horses are replaced by coconut shells!

One of the tragedies of the Reformation era was the overreaction to medieval abuses which led the radical reformers to throw out the baby with the bath water (or baptismal water, if you happen to be Quaker). Because *things* and *stuff* had been sorely misused, some of the radical Protestants decided to just do away with everything physical: no more stained glass, statues, incense, bread, wine - no more symbols at all. But humans were created by God to be symbolic creatures. The only way we communicate is through symbols. Full-orbed worship will include the use of wood and wax, and even bells and banners, all gloriously transformed into the symbols of the drama which we present to God (who, after all, obviously loves this stuff - just read his commands regarding worship in the Tabernacle and Temple, and read about worship in heaven in the book of Revelation). In Christ, the created world is redeemed and is used for his glory. Matter matters.

Great actors don't just walk on stage unprepared. They sometimes spend a long time getting in character - getting into the role. In Chapter Twelve we will look at developing a sacramental way of thinking, a biblical mindset that recovers the use of *things* in the worship of God.

The Climax

There are some dramas (you can't really even call them dramas - they are "experimental theater"), from which you walk away and don't have a clue what just happened. I suppose there are also some church services like that! A good drama has a climax - it has a point to which everything is building. It usually appears in the last (or next to the last) act, and it brings resolution to the entire piece. In Christian worship this climax, this pinnacle of the production, is called the Eucharist (from which, by the way, the whole play takes its name - "The Great Thanksgiving").

Act Three of the drama of worship is when we proclaim again the amazing story of our redemption in Christ Jesus, and when we actually participate in that moment of his supreme sacrifice for us. When we receive Holy Communion we are being graced with the very true and real presence of Jesus in our own bodies, souls and spirits, and we are also offering to the Father thanksgiving and praise for the once-for-all, totally sufficient sacrifice of Jesus on the cross.

In Chapters Thirteen and Fourteen we will give special attention to the Sacraments - those physical/spiritual means by which we offer thanksgiving to God, and through which we receive grace and mercy.

It's A Wrap

When the drama of worship is finished, when the command performance for the King is done, the story doesn't end. The King, who has called us to offer this great thanksgiving, is just thrilled by our act of true worship. If you can imagine, he stands up and applauds and with every clap of his hands waves of blessings roll out over the cast and crew. Then we go out to live the drama before our friends and neighbors and to take the Good News we have been celebrating to the whole world. And then we come back and do it again. For the joy set before us.

If you are a baptized Christian, you are already a member of the cast. This book is to help you get to know your fellow cast members (the Church), to introduce you to the acts (the liturgy), to give you an overview of the script (the Bible), and to help you understand the climax of the drama (the Sacraments). So find a comfortable chair, warm up a cup of coffee, get your pen ready to make some notes, and let's begin. Break a leg.

Chapter One

Meet The Troupe:
The Church Defined

You've saved your money, planned your trip, and now the day arrives. You've bought special tickets for the Broadway production of *Les Miserables* and you have the best seats in the house. But when you get to the theater the doors are closed because the actors guild is on strike. There will be no play tonight because there are no actors. You can go back to your hotel room and read the book on which the play is based (well, not in one night, you can't), or you can rent the video and watch the movie. But neither experience is the same as seeing the thing on stage. And the simple truth is, without the actors there is no play.

In this grand drama of our redemption, this great celebration of God's love toward us in Jesus Christ, this fantastic service of thanksgiving, if there is no troupe of actors there is no production. Beginning with Adam, moving forward through Abraham and Moses and David and the people of Israel, and continuing through Jesus and the Apostles and the New Testament Christians, God has been raising up a company of performers, and that company is called *the Church*.

Let's All Do Our Civic Duty

When Jesus turned to Simon Peter and said, "And I tell you that you are Peter, and on this rock I will build my *church*, and the gates of Hades will not overcome it" (Matthew 16.18), he used an astonishing word. He could have said, "I will build my synagogue," or "I will build my temple," or "I will build my religion," but instead he reached into the Greco-Roman world and pulled out a word with a completely different meaning: *ekklesia*.

When we say the word "church" today we tend to think of a building, or a group of people, or a denomination. And when we see that Greek word used in English words (like *ecclesiastical*) we think of "things pertaining to religion." But when Jesus first said it, he said something startling. The Greek word *ekklesia* doesn't mean a religious gathering or group. It comes from the political world of the Greeks and Romans, and it literally means a *called out group*. The common meaning in Jesus' time was a civic gathering. The emperor or his representative would send word to the citizens of a city and "call them out" for a special meeting or task. Jesus was not saying "I will build my religious institution," he was saying, "I will build my new nation, my new citizenship." What he said did not stand over against the synagogue, it stood over against the political systems of the world, be they Roman or Jewish. Jesus was ushering in a new *kingdom*, and the people of the kingdom were called the *ecclesia*, the *Church*.[1]

To be fair, Jesus wasn't the first Jew to use this term. In the Greek Old Testament (the *Septuagint*) the word is used over 100 times, and in every case it "is a wholly secular term."[2] It means "the assembly": "I will declare your name to my brothers," David said, "in the *congregation* [*ekklesia*] I will praise you" (Psalm

---

[1] For a detailed study of the word, cf. Kittel, Gerhard, *Theological Dictionary of the New Testament*, Volume III, pp. 501-536; Grand Rapids, MI; Eerdmans Publishing Company, 1965.

[2] *ibid*, p. 527.

22.22). In the Old Testament, the "congregation" meant the whole political body of Israel, and not the people who showed up in synagogue on the Sabbath.

In the New Testament the word comes into its own. It is the new *community* of people who follow Jesus Christ as Lord, as Governor, as King. In Matthew's gospel Jesus promised to build his Church, and promised that the powers of hell would not be able to stand in the way of its progress, but this community was not fully born until the Day of Pentecost, when the Holy Spirit was given and the Church was "birthed" (Acts 2).

A Rose By Any Other Name

Throughout the writings of the Apostles this company of the Kingdom is called by several other names, each adding an insight into the calling and purpose of the Church. Here are a few descriptive titles:

> • **The Body of Christ**: And God placed all things under his feet and appointed him to be head over everything for the church, which is his body, the fullness of him who fills everything in every way (Ephesians 1.22f).

• **The Bride of Christ**: I saw the Holy City, the new Jerusalem, coming down out of heaven from God, prepared as a bride beautifully dressed for her husband (Revelation 21.2).

• **The Flock**: Be shepherds of God's flock that is under your care, serving as overseers (1 Peter 5.2).

• **God's Household**: Consequently, you are no longer foreigners and aliens, but fellow citizens with God's people and members of God's household (Ephesians 2.19).

• **A Spiritual House**: You also, like living stones, are being built into a spiritual house to be a holy priesthood (1 Peter 2.5).

• **The Temple**: For we are the temple of the living God (2 Corinthians 6.16).

• **The Chosen People, Royal Priesthood, Holy Nation**: But you are a chosen people, a royal priesthood, a holy nation, a people belonging to God, that you may declare the praises of him who called you out of darkness into his wonderful light. Once you were not a people, but now you are the people of God; once you had not received mercy, but now you have received mercy (1 Peter 2.9-10).

Put them all together and you get the idea of the immensity of this thing. The Church is the people of God who are called out by him to be an eternal counterpart to the kingdoms of this world.

Will the Real Church Please Stand Up?

The Eastern Orthodox churches see themselves (and rightly so) as being in continuity with the churches established by the Apostles themselves. Think about it: there is a Christian presence in Ephesus to this day; and in Antioch, and in Corinth (modern day Selçuk, Antakya and Korinthos, respectively) - and these Eastern Orthodox churches have an unbroken lineage that stretches all the way back to their foundation by the Apostles. So when the Orthodox speak of other churches not in communion with them, they are careful not to pass judgment. Instead they say, "We know where the Church is, but we are not sure where the Church is not." In other words, they are convinced that Orthodoxy is the Church, but what else is also the Church they cannot be sure. This allows the Orthodox to claim to be the true Church without actually denying that the true Church is also to be found elsewhere.

Having said that, not everything that calls itself "the Church" is the Church. There are cults and heresies which call themselves the Church, and yet which also deny the basic Christian faith. What, then, constitutes the Church? What are the marks of the true Church?

The Protestant List of Three

In the Protestant tradition, birthed in the sixteenth century era of Martin Luther, and including practically every church in Western Christianity except the Roman Catholic Church, it has been understood that there are three basic ingredients which constitute the Church.

First, the preaching of God's Word. It was the very Word of God that formed the Church to begin with. Remember, the Church is the "called out people" who have responded to the call of a herald. Jesus, the Word made flesh, came among us and preached the Kingdom of God. The Apostles took that message to the ends of the earth, and the people who respond to that message, who live by it and cherish it, are the Church; they are, indeed, people of the Word.

Second, the administration of God's Sacraments. Jesus himself commanded the disciples to baptize, and to celebrate Holy Communion "in remembrance" of him. The Church is evidenced by a faithful continuance of these sacraments.

Third, the discipline of God's people. Jesus told the Twelve to "go and make disciples" of the nations (Matthew 28.18). There is a moral and ethical dimension to being the called out people of God; there is a behavioral response to being chosen by God. The final mark of this famous Protestant triad is that its leadership is to exercise authority in calling the people to live godly lives.

This triad has been referred to as the three legged stool of the Church, and it is a good beginning. But if the Protestant tradition has a three legged stool, the Catholic tradition has a four legged stool. In the next chapter we will explore together the four ancient marks of the Church.

Chapter Two

The Actors' Guild:
The Historic Qualities Of The Church

In the previous chapter we saw that the Church is "the called out people of God," a group of people who have responded to the call of faith in and faithfulness to Jesus Christ. The Church, called by many names in the New Testament, has been defined (in Protestant circles) as existing wherever three things are present: the Word of God faithfully preached, the Sacraments of God faithfully celebrated, and the discipline of God faithfully administered.

Now we come to an even older marking which gives definition to the Church in its fullness. In the Nicene Creed we confess, "I believe one, holy, catholic and apostolic Church." This ancient creed (fourth century A.D.) is universally accepted as a statement of Christian truth, but the individual words used to define the Church - one, holy, catholic and apostolic - are older still.[3]

One

Jesus wanted his Church to be one. Some churches make the claim that it *is* one, because they are the only true Church and if you aren't part of them you aren't part of the Church. But wait - didn't Jesus *pray* for his Church to *be* one? Didn't he ask of the Father that the Church "*be brought* to complete unity" (John 17.23)? And isn't the implication of Jesus' prayer that, at best, there is the *possibility* of disunity, and at worst, that such disunity actually exists? Read again the words that Jesus prayed for the Church:

> My prayer is not for them alone
> [*the Twelve*]. I pray also for those
> who will believe in me through
> their message, that all of them may

[3] For a fuller treatment of this phrase from the Nicene Creed see Chapter 10 in my *What Christians Believe*; Sherman, TX, Mayeux Press, 2009.

be one, Father, just as you are in me
and I am in you. May they also be
in us so that the world may believe
that you have sent me. I have given
them the glory that you gave me,
that they may be one as we are one:
I in them and you in me. May they
be brought to complete unity to let
the world know that you sent me
and have loved them even as you
have loved me (John 17.20-23).

How can we possibly say that one of
the historic marks of the Church is that it is
one, when to all appearances, it is no sort of
thing? Well, for starters, it *was* just this sort of
thing in the beginning. Have you ever thought
about the amazing level of unity in the Church
during the first few centuries? Consider just
the first century. The early Church was
birthed under intense persecution. All but one
of the original disciples died a violent death.
People were driven from their cities, fired
from their jobs, stoned, starved and
scandalized just for being Christians. Through
either an evangelistic zeal or as the result of
persecution, within 40 years of Jesus' death
the Church had been established on three
continents, worship was being held in at least
half a dozen different languages, and countless
cultures had been transcended by the Gospel.

At this point there was no New Testament - no leather bound set of the writings of the Apostles, nor were there any kind of developed canons or constitutions or bylaws for governing the Church. And yet - here is the astonishing thing - and yet, in all these different cultures, on all these different continents, in all these different languages, the same faith and doctrine was believed, the same structure of leadership was in place, and the same form of worship was occurring!

In spite of the emerging early heresies (when people were claiming to be the Church but were actually twisting off from the true faith), the New Covenant people of God were, against all odds, *one*. And although there were fierce theological and spiritual battles to be fought in the coming centuries, the Church remained one for the first thousand years of her existence!

But surely she isn't one anymore, someone might exclaim, and on a surface level that someone would be correct. The Great Schism of 1054 saw a terrible division between the Eastern and Western Churches. The Reformation of the 16th Century saw even more splintering. Today, with something like 25,000 denominations in existence, it is easy to say the church most assuredly is *not* one. All is not well in Christiantown. Jesus' prayer *needs* to be answered by the Father, and it needs to be prayed by believers.

And yet, in a deeper spiritual sense, that unity still exists. While the Roman Catholic, Eastern Orthodox, Anglican, Methodist, Baptist, Pentecostal, and Non-denominational churches (and all the rest that I don't have room to mention) are very different in their practices, doctrines, and disciplines, there is still an underlying unity, particularly in two things.

There is a unity of faith in Jesus Christ as Lord and Savior, and there is a unity in the basic Christian doctrines as expressed in the Creeds (even churches that never say the Creeds still believe what the Creeds affirm).

When we say that the Church is one, in that deeper spiritual sense, we are not pretending that divisions do not exist. The unity is not, as Jesus prayed, "complete." The divisions that exist in the Body of Christ are not pleasing to God, and part of the work that Christians should be committed to is the long and hard work of transcending the barriers that divide us, not by shallow compromise, but by a dedicated commitment to recovering the faith and practice of the ancient undivided

Church. This work is made easier by the moving of the Holy Spirit, who in our own generation has done so much to tear down the walls between believing brothers and sisters.

Holy

Simply put, the word holy means *unique*. It goes hand in hand with the idea of being a called out people. In the book of Ephesians the Apostle Paul writes of this holiness:

> Consequently, you are no longer foreigners and aliens, but fellow citizens with God's people and members of God's household, built on the foundation of the apostles and prophets, with Christ Jesus himself as the chief cornerstone. In him the whole building is joined together and rises to become a *holy* temple in the Lord (Ephesians 2.19-21).

> Husbands, love your wives, just as Christ loved the church and gave himself up for her to make her *holy*, cleansing her by the washing with water through the word, and to

present her to himself as a radiant church, without stain or wrinkle or any other blemish, but *holy* and blameless (Ephesians 5.25-27).

In the Church, God is doing something *different*, something *unique*, from the rest of the world; the Church is the beginning of his new creation, his restoration of all things (Acts 3.21ff).

Holiness has been given a bad rap in our day. It has been misdefined as legalism. Nothing could be further from the truth. When the Bible speaks of being holy the idea is of being *separate, other than*. The King James Version calls us "a peculiar people" (1 Peter 2.9). Peculiar doesn't mean weird (though as a young man I actually heard it preached that this was precisely what the Bible meant, and therefore Christians had to wear their hair, clothing, and make-up [or lack thereof] different from those around them). When the KJV translators used the word, peculiar meant *singular*. The idea isn't to be strange, but to be unique.

The Bride of Christ is defined by her differentness from the world; we live by God's standards, not the fallen world's; we hold to the values of heaven, not the values of our particular culture and age. Holiness, then, is best understood as being faithful to God's revealed will as found in Holy Scriptures. Much of modern religion has sought to make the faith palatable to the society which surrounds it. In doing so there has been a dilution of God's will and an accommodation to sub-biblical norms. The mistake has been this: rather than a fresh *application* of God's Word to society, there has been a *reinterpretation* of God's word, catering to society. One important mark of the Church has always been that she is *other than* the world around her. She breathes different air. She breathes the air of heaven. She is holy.

Catholic

I began my ministry as an assistant pastor in a church founded and pastored by my father-in-law, in the Texas border town of Zapata. There were (and are) lots of Hispanics there, and lots of Roman Catholics. Sadly, in the parlance of the day, when Roman Catholics and Protestants dialogued, one would say, "I'm Catholic, not Christian," and the other would say, "I'm Christian, not Catholic." Yikes! Both were wrong. In the strictest sense of the words, one cannot be Christian without also being Catholic, and one cannot be Catholic without also being Christian.

The word catholic is one of the earliest words used to describe the Church. It was used for the first time by a man who was ordained by the Apostles themselves. Get the history clear in your mind: Ignatius was born sometime between A.D. 35 and 50. As a young man he was friends with John the Apostle. Peter, who founded the church in Antioch, personally appointed Ignatius as its bishop. He was friends with the other students of the Apostles, and he was a contemporary of Timothy and Titus. My point is, Ignatius (whom I am about to quote) was no johnny-come-lately. He died a martyr, fed to the lions in Rome in the year 112, not a dozen years after John died. OK, just so you have it straight: you can't get any closer to the Apostles themselves than Ignatius. And it was Ignatius who first used the word catholic regarding the Church: "Wherever the bishop appears, the whole congregation is to be present, just as wherever Jesus Christ is, there is the *Catholic Church*" (Smyrneans 8.2).

"But what does it *mean*?" you may be shouting by now. It is a Greek phrase, *kath' holou*, which means "of the whole." Not unlike DNA, in which the whole code of the body can be found in any particular cell of the body, the word catholic implies that the fullness of the Church can be found in any "cell" of the Church (a cell being the nucleus of a bishop surrounded by those who accompany him in the faith). For Ignatius and the early Christians, anywhere the people of God gathered in unity around a bishop in apostolic succession (more about this in Chapter Four), there was the presence of the whole Church - the little cell was integrally connected to, at one with, and part of the larger whole, and the larger whole was also mysteriously contained in that little gathering.

Being catholic has several implications, including three very important ones. First, the Church is inclusive. It is for everyone. The Church cannot be catholic and reject people because of race, gender, culture or nationality. When a church refuses someone on the basis of his skin color or social status, it loses its catholicity.

Second, the Church is interdependent. There really can be no such thing as an independent church. The very phrase is an oxymoron, a contradiction of terms. If the Church is catholic, it is not locally independent, but is simply a local expression of the universal (in time and place) Body of

Christ. There is, therefore, a responsibility for the individual believer and the local congregation to heed the rest of the Church.

Third, the Church is nonsectarian. It is not distinguished by a particular doctrine, practice or philosophy. That we all have labels is a sad commentary on the state of the Church today. Ideally we should not be identified as Roman, Orthodox, Anglican, Baptist, Pentecostal or any of the other distinctives which we use to identify ourselves. Even if we are identified as such, this certainly should not be the spirit in which we present ourselves. There should never be an "us vs. them" attitude in the Church. We are all called to be *fully* and *wholly* Christian, that is, catholic - of the whole.

Apostolic

The final ancient mark of the Church is that it is apostolic, that is, from the Apostles. Anything and everything we as Christians have received comes from and is rooted in the lives, authority and teaching of the Apostles. It is simply impossible to be Christian without them as our foundation (cf. Ephesians 2.20, Revelation 21.14). There are three areas in which apostolicity should be measured in the Church.

First, the Church is apostolic in its doctrine. We must hold the same teachings which the Apostles held and transmitted to others. This is found primarily in the New Testament, but also in the tradition of the ancient Church. I find it interesting (and sometimes amusing) that some independent minded churches insist that they have nothing to do with "tradition", and yet they base everything they believe on the New Testament. Where in the world do they think those 27 books came from? *Who says* those 27 are the Word of God? Why not 29? Why not 22? Why those particular ones? How about we throw out Hebrews because we don't like it, or maybe the book of Revelation? The truth is, anyone who trusts in the canon of the New Testament is, whether he admits it or not, also trusting in the *tradition* of the Church. For the first four centuries there was no New Testament. It was canonized in the fifth century. In Church Councils. By a bunch of bishops. Catholic bishops. Lest you think I've gone off on a rabbit trail, let me bring this to a point: any church which embraces the canon of Scripture as the Word of God is, whether it realizes it or not, embracing not only the authority of the Apostles, but also the authority of ancient tradition in direct descent from the Apostles. To be apostolic is to embrace apostolic doctrine, *delivered to us through the Church*.

Second, the Church is apostolic in its practice. This means doing what the Apostles did. Certainly this includes the ethics and morals of the Apostles, based on their witness in Holy Scriptures, but it also includes their spiritual life of prayer, their being used in the power of the Holy Spirit, and their worship of God. We as Christians in the Church have a responsibility to mimic the lives, actions, values and practices of the Apostles, who themselves followed the life, actions, values and practices of Jesus Christ. Paul told the church in Corinth, "Therefore I urge you to imitate me" (1 Corinthians 4.16). He told them, "Follow my example, as I follow the example of Christ" (1 Corinthians 11.1).

Third, the Church is apostolic in its succession. A church that is apostolic in the full sense should also be apostolic in its line of authority - that is, there should be an unbroken transmission of authority from the Apostles to the present leaders. Just as Paul ordained Timothy and then directed him to ordain other trustworthy men who would succeed him, the continuity of ministerial authority continues to this very day. Having said that, there are bishops and priests who may technically claim apostolic succession, but who have abandoned apostolic doctrine and practice. Succession alone does not bring full apostolicity. To be fully catholic is to be fully apostolic - succession, doctrine and practice.

With so many different groups and denominations - with so many streams - it would be true to say that the Church is faithful to these four marks *in varying degrees*. But our goal should be to work toward a fullness of these qualities "until," as Saint Paul wrote, "we all reach unity in the faith and in the knowledge of the Son of God and become mature, attaining to the whole measure of the fullness of Christ" (Ephesians 4.13).

Chapter Three

The Show Must Go On:
The Church's Purpose

So here we all are, gathered onto a stage in an empty theater, a troupe of actors who have been together for years and know each other intimately. We've done everything from William Shakespeare to Andrew Lloyd Webber. What are we doing now? Before a troupe can spring into action, before it can even begin preparing, it must know its purpose. Why is it here? What is its task? What is expected of it?

As a pastor, I can't tell you how many times I have been approached by people asking me to help them discover their purpose in life. But, like a soldier in a battle, you can't really discover your personal purpose without seeing it in the larger context of the purpose of your fellow soldiers - your squad, or regiment, or battalion. The answer to "What am *I* supposed to do?" is contained in the answer to, "What are *we* supposed to do?" The first question cannot be accurately answered until the correct answer is discovered for the second question.

Purpose is a very *personal* thing, but it is not an *individual* thing. God has created each one of us uniquely fit for his purposes, and our own personal calling should relate to the larger calling of the Church - all his people together. What, then, is the purpose of the Church of God? I suppose a hundred things could be listed, but we will settle for four, and these will be presented in ascending order - from the least to the most important (not that the least is unimportant - the least is *very* important, just not as important as the most. Got it? Good). Before looking at the four purposes of the Church, we need to see the bigger picture of the context in which the Church exists.

The Big Picture

The Church of God cannot be understood apart from the Kingdom of God, because the Church is the people of the Kingdom. The Kingdom of God (or the Kingdom of Heaven) is the central theme of the Bible. It has, in much of Christianity, been hijacked and replaced by the theme of "When you die, do you know where you would spend eternity?," but that question is never asked by the Prophets, Jesus or the Apostles. It is only asked by well-meaning and sincere modern Christians who might well not realize the *real* central theme of Scripture. And it's not a *bad* question, it's just not *the* question.

What the prophets proclaimed was the promise of an arriving Kingdom of God which was prefigured (albeit sinfully and often poorly) in the nation of Israel, birthed in the life of Jesus Christ and expanded in the ministry of the early Church.

The Kingdom of God was the central focus of Jesus' earthly ministry. From his incarnation to his ascension, the thirty three years of his life were consumed with the Kingdom of God.

He came to proclaim its nearness: "From that time on Jesus began to preach, 'Repent, for the kingdom of heaven is near'" (Matthew 4.17).

He came to usher in its presence: "But if I drive out demons by the Spirit of God, then the kingdom of God has come upon you" (Matthew 12.28).

He came to teach its principles: "Blessed are the poor in Spirit, for theirs is the kingdom of heaven" (Matthew 5.3).

When we think of a kingdom today, we tend to think of geography - the Kingdom of Saudi Arabia, for example, or the Kingdom of England (yes, England *was* a Kingdom, for nearly 1000 years). In our minds, a kingdom is primarily defined by its borders. But the biblical word (*basileia*) denotes not so much borders as influence. The Kingdom of God is *dynamic*. It is not so much a territory as it is a living rule or reign. Maybe *that's* a better way to say it - "the Reign of God." The Kingdom of God is anywhere (and that could be in an individual's life, in a family, a church, a nation, or even the whole world) where God's reign is received, enjoyed and lived under. It carries with it certain loyalties, governing principles, blessings and powers which are not to be found outside the Kingdom.

What Christ came to establish was not just the Church, but the Reign of God. The Church is the community of that reign - the people who live by the precepts and enjoy the benefits of Christ's rule. As such, the Church's purpose is always to be found in relation to its being the Kingdom People.

A Witnessing Community

As the People of God, we stand in relationship not only to our Sovereign, our Lord, God Almighty; we also stand in relationship to other people - even to the nations as a whole. The Apostles spent and gave their lives in order to testify to others about the good news of the Kingdom of God. Within its first thirty years, the early church mushroomed from a handful of believers in Jerusalem to a network of congregations found throughout the entire known world. By the year A.D. 70 the Kingdom of God had been testified to and brought to such far flung places as Britain, Ethiopia and India. Gatherings of Kingdom citizens loyal to the lordship of Jesus could be found not only in Jerusalem, but in Tunis, Tunisia (Carthage), Guruvayoor, India (Palayoor), Glastonbury, England, and innumerable cities and towns in between. And this is within *the first thirty years* of our history! From that time, the Reign of Christ has been brought, through the witness of missionaries and evangelists and regular folk, to every corner of the world, and though there are ups and downs, progress and setbacks, wins and losses, the promise of the Scripture is that the Kingdom of God will continue to expand until true and godly worship is offered in every place from the rising to the setting of the sun, and until all nations walk in the light of the glory of God:

> Malachi 1.11: "My name will be great among the nations, from the rising to the setting of the sun. In every place incense and pure offerings will be brought to my name, because my name will be great among the nations," says the Lord Almighty.

> Isaiah 11.9: For the earth will be full of the knowledge of the Lord as the waters cover the sea.

> Matthew 28.18-20: Then Jesus came to them and said, "All authority in heaven and on earth has been given to me. Therefore go and make disciples of all nations, baptizing them in the name of the Father and of the Son and of the Holy Spirit, and teaching them to obey everything I have commanded you. And surely I am with you always, to the very end of the age."

A Working Community

Not only is the Church called to witness to the world (not, mind you, to offer a fire-insurance plan for eternity, but to transform the nations both here and hereafter), it also has other work to do. Jesus said to his disciples, "As long as it is day, we must do the *work* of him who sent me" (John 9.4), and that work continues throughout the history of the Church.

When Paul and Barnabas were set aside for their missionary task (which happened, by the way, while the Church leaders in Antioch were "worshiping" - literally, "performing their liturgy"), the Holy Spirit said, "Set apart for me Barnabas and Saul for the *work* to which I have called them" (Acts 13.2). Later, when this same Apostle Paul wrote to the Church in Corinth, he said, "Therefore my dear brothers, stand firm. Let nothing move you. Always give yourselves fully to the *work* of the Lord, because you know that your labor in the Lord is not in vain" (1 Corinthians 15.58).

You see, then, that the believer is not brought into the Kingdom of God simply to "get saved" and then get on with life. We are saved to accomplish the ongoing work of *expanding* the Kingdom of God. This expansion is indeed spiritual, but it is much more than "just" spiritual - it calls for the evangelization of the world, the transformation of society, the care of God's creation. It means that every believer, whatever his job, does it for the glory of God. Being a nurse can be every bit as spiritual as being a priest. Being a carpenter, or barber, or secretary, or factory worker, or homemaker is every bit as much Kingdom work as being clergy. The Church's task is to bring the Reign of God to bear in everyday life: personal, social, religious, artistic, governmental - in short, in *every* aspect of life.

A Winning Community

Our work is not for naught. Unfortunately, some Christians have embraced a mindset that says we all lose in the here and now. The world, we are told, is going to hell in a handbasket, so the best we can hope for is to rescue a few souls from the sinking ship of planet Earth. The Church, we are told, is destined to be a remnant, a few faithful holding on to the end, waiting for rescue. All our witnessing and all our working, we are told, has only minimal success. We don't *really* succeed, we are told, until after the fact, after history comes to a close.

The Bible teaches otherwise. Whatever your understanding is about the future, one thing should be scripturally clear: the Church is called to win, both in this world and in the world to come.

When Simon had the revelation that Jesus was the Son of the Living God, Jesus responded to him and said, "And I tell you that you are Peter, and on this rock I will build my church, and the gates of hell *will not overcome it*" (Matthew 15.18). Think, just for a minute, about what a gate is. Gates don't go forward into battle; gates are defensive. They are stationary. It is the Church that moves forward in battle, and hell's gates cannot withstand it. In the Old Testament, the governing bodies of cities met "at the city gate" to discuss politics. And so, the gates of a place represented the authority of the place. The authority of hell cannot withstand the authority of the Kingdom of God. This is a promise from our King himself.

Saint Paul picked up this theme in his epistles when he wrote to the Church in Rome to encourage it. No matter what obstacles we face, he wrote - no matter what adversaries align against God's people - "in all these things we are *more than conquerors* through him who loved us" (Romans 8.37). Later, when he wrote to the little struggling Church in the pagan city of Corinth, he told them, "But thanks be to God, who always leads us in *triumphal procession* in Christ and through us spreads everywhere the fragrance of the knowledge of him" (2 Corinthians 2.14).

The old man and last surviving member of the Apostolic team - Saint John - wrote to the people under his care, "You, dear children, are from God and have *overcome* them, because *the one who is in you is greater than the one who is in the world*...for everyone born of God *overcomes* the world. This is the *victory* that has *overcome* the world, even our faith. Who is it that *overcomes* the world? Only he who believes that Jesus is the Son of God" (1 John 4.4, 5.4f). The promise of Jesus and the declaration of the Apostles is not that if we hang on long enough God will send a rescue party, but that if we endure in the work he has called us to, we will win.

A Worshiping Community

I told you we were doing this in ascending order. Think of our discussion as moving from the outside inward, from the bottom of a broad hill up to the pinnacle. We are a witnessing community - reaching out to those outside the Church and bringing them in; we are a working community - living our own lives under the Rule of Christ; we are a winning community - actually accomplishing (albeit through battle) the tasks set before us by our King; but most important, we are a worshiping community, called to offer the service of worship to our Lord and God. In the life of the believer and in the life of the Church, *nothing is as important as worship*.

When Jesus was asked what was the most important commandment of all, he quoted Deuteronomy 6.5: "Love the Lord your God with all your heart and with all your soul and with all your strength" (cf. Matthew 22.34-39). The single most important thing we do as believers in Christ is to love him and worship him. When Moses delivered the Ten Commandments to the people of Israel (Exodus 20), the first and foremost was that God's people would worship God and serve him only.

All other works and ministries flow from our work of worship. An ancient rule of the Church was *lex orandi lex credendi* - "What we pray is what we believe," or "praying shapes believing." Taken a step further, what we believe is how we act - believing shapes doing. In other words, our praying to God (and the greater context of our worshiping God) shapes everything else about our Christian walk. Everything - our beliefs, our actions, our values, our attitudes, our working, our living - flows from our worship.

Worshiping God creates a sphere in which God's Spirit can extend God's rule and reign. The Psalmist wrote, "Yet you are holy, enthroned on the praises of Israel" (Psalm 22.3). God is enthroned on the praise of his people. He is established as King when his people worship him.

Ready the Troops, Ready the Troupe

The last couple of sections have had a military undertone to them - we are warriors of God, troops on the battlefield pressing toward victory. But let's take the analogy back to the world of drama, shall we? We are a troupe, performing the act - the play, the drama - of worship. Our victory is rooted in our worship of the King. It is from this that everything else springs.

Having established that the Church's primary purpose is to worship God, the rest of this book is about *how* we worship. One word of explanation before we move on: there is little in these pages about personal devotion or private piety. There is scant reference to our individual frame of mind or our personal spirituality. These things are important, but these are not the focus of this book. There is also very little here about musical styles or charismatic activity. This is a manual for the actor's guild - to introduce them and teach them and remind them of the show, the command performance, they are celebrating before our King. Other troupes cover Shakespeare and Ibsen. We do the Divine Liturgy - the drama of our redemption - the greatest show on earth.

Chapter Four

Who's Running This Show?
Leadership in Apostolic Succession

I'm writing this chapter while sitting on a beautiful covered patio outside my room at a hotel in Merida, Yucatan, Mexico. I have actually written three of the four books in this series at this same hotel because it is an excellent place to escape the hustle and bustle of everyday life and ministry, a place to think and be creative. In between chapters my wife and I can walk a few blocks to the central plaza and find wonderful outdoor cafes for lunch and dinner. The city of Merida was founded in 1542 and is home to the oldest cathedral on the western continents. On every corner, it seems, is a gorgeous church or palace or government hall which invites the passersby to stop for a moment and look up and take in all the beauty of the architecture.

I'm not telling you this to make you envious or to brag about where I am. I have a point to make, and here it is: every one of these buildings took teamwork to build, and each one of them required some kind of master plan and someone with authority to execute that plan. I wonder what the Catedral de San Ildefonso would look like if folk had just gotten together and said, "Hey, let's build a church," with no plan, and no one in charge of construction. Goodness! There might not even be a straight line or a connecting hallway in the whole place, let alone any kind of symmetry or style or beauty. It would be chaos, and it would be, mostly, nonfunctional. God is a God of order, and he has created a world of order and he has made humans as a people with order innately built into their psyches.[4]

When it comes to everything else in life, we insist on order and structure: we want our eggs cooked a certain way; we want our music to be harmonious; we want our highway traffic to flow without disruption. We never stop to

---

[4] If you don't believe me, just research Fibonacci numbers and the Golden Mean.

think that for our eggs and music and highways to "work," someone has to be in charge. Someone has to have the authority to tell others what to do and how to do it. But when it comes to church, a lot of Christians rile up at the thought of there being anyone with any kind of real or true authority. Some people like to imagine the church as a conglomeration of members who each have a vote on how things are done and the majority rules. Others see pastors as hirelings who do the bidding of the congregation or the board. Some even go so far as to say, "We have no leadership and no one in authority, we are just led by the Spirit."

Even in congregations which *are* locally ordered and structured, oftentimes church structure has been mistakenly understood in two ways, each of which may be compared to a particular form of sea life. The first is the single-cell amoeba which, though highly structured within itself, is responsible and accountable to no one else. The independent church movement tends to look at each congregation as completely autonomous, choosing its own course of spiritual life and doctrine, without reference to any other structure.

The second is like a jellyfish: a loosely structured grouping of cells (and even individual organisms) which float along as a bobbing blob. In some denominations the structure of leadership is at best minimal, and certainly is not viewed as essential to the life and direction of the church.

Interestingly, churches with these personalities tend to attract people with these personalities. So an independent-minded church may be filled with independent-minded people who have difficulty working together for the betterment of the Kingdom.

Fortunately, there is a biblical and historic model of structure for the Church. Not only has it endured for two thousand years, it is also of apostolic design.

The Priesthood of All Believers

Before anything is said about hierarchy or leadership, it is important to lay the groundwork that, in order to fulfill the ministry of the Church (witness, work, winning, worship), God has chosen to *ordain every believer* into a priesthood called to accomplish these purposes. Our baptism serves, among other things, as an ordination into the common Christian priesthood.

There are two words in the New Testament which get translated into the English word *priest*. The first is *hieros*, and it literally means "one who cuts," that is, "one who makes sacrifices." Now, here is the important thing about this word as it is used by the Apostles: it *always* refers to the whole people of God and *never* refers to a special group within the Church. In other words, when the transition was made between an Old Testament caste of priests who made sacrifices of animals (Levites and sons of Aaron and *not* all Jews) and the New Testament writings about priests, the company of sacrificers is expanded to include all believers!

Saint Peter wrote, to the whole Church, "You also, like living stones, are being built into a spiritual house to be *a holy priesthood*...you are *a royal priesthood*, a holy nation, a people belonging to God..." (1 Peter 2.5,9). If we are all priests (and the Bible says we are), and if there is now no sacrifice of the blood of bulls and goats to be offered, what is the sacrifice we make? In the same text, Saint Peter tells us, "...to be a holy priesthood, *offering spiritual sacrifices*...a royal priesthood...that you may *declare the praises* of him who has called you out of darkness into his wonderful light." Christians, acting together as an holy priesthood, offer the spiritual sacrifice of praise and thanksgiving to God. The writer of Hebrews instructs us, "Through Jesus, therefore, let us continually offer to God *a sacrifice of praise* - the fruit of lips that confess his name" (Hebrews 13.15).

So we are clear that what we're talking about here is not just lip service, but life service, Saint Paul reminds us, "in view of God's mercy, to *offer your bodies as a living sacrifice*, holy and pleasing to God - this is your *spiritual act of worship*." As the old "General Thanksgiving" says, "we show forth thy praise, not only with our lips, but in our lives, by giving up ourselves to thy service, and by walking before thee in holiness and righteousness all our days..."

Our Christian work, our Christian sacrifice, our priestly duty, therefore, is to praise God. Together. As a company of priests. As a congregation of people. As a troupe of holy actors acting out the story of our salvation. And this act is *chiefly* done in what is called *The Great Thanksgiving*, when we come together to proclaim God's Word and feast at his Table; when we come to confess our faith and *participate* in Christ's once and for all sacrifice of his body and blood for the life of the world.

Ordained Leadership

"Whoopie! We are *all* priests," I can hear it now, "and I don't need anyone to tell me how to serve my God!" But wait just a minute! Even the Reformers, who rediscovered that missing jewel of a doctrine, the priesthood of all believers, which had long laid covered over with the dust of medieval clericalism, were careful to make this distinction: it is the priesthood of *all* believers, not the priesthood of *each* believer. We are not offering so many million or billion one-man plays. We are offering epic theater of our thanksgiving. This is not Hal Holbrook doing *Mark Twain*, a single figure on the stage. This is Cecil B. DeMille and "a cast of thousands" doing *The Ten Commandments* - working *together* to create an astonishing production.

And speaking of Cecil B. DeMille, let me mention a few more names in that vein: Fellini; Spielberg; Lucas; Tarantino; Scorsese; Hitchcock - directors who are household names. You may not like what they've done, but you must admit that they are masters in their field. Someone obviously likes what they have done - a lot of someones, in fact. Every great movie and every great play has a great

director. In the Church, although the entire
cast of believers is a priesthood, and the entire
drama is a sacrifice of praise, God has
appointed leadership to direct, and he has
appointed some among us for the lead roles.
Biblically and historically, leadership falls into
three offices.

Bishops   The Apostles appointed and
ordained men to continue their apostolic role
of oversight and called them *episkopos* or
bishops. The Greek word literally means
overseer (*epi* = over; *skopos* = to see [*a la*
telescope, periscope, and microscope]). As
early as Acts 20, when Paul set in place
spiritual leadership in Ephesus, we read,
"Keep watch over yourselves and all the flock
of which the Holy Spirit has made you
overseers" (Acts 20.28). Later Paul would write
to the Church in Philippi, "Paul and Timothy,
servants of Christ Jesus. To all the saints in
Christ at Philippi, together with the *overseers*
and deacons" (Philippians 1.1). When Paul
gave his young protege Timothy (himself a
bishop ordained by Paul) instructions for
establishing the Church he admonished him,
"If anyone sets his heart on being an *overseer*,
he desires a noble task" (1 Timothy 3.1).

That first generation of bishops are
names spoken with reverence by those who

know their legacy: Timothy, Titus, Clement, Polycarp, Ignatius - men ordained by the Apostles themselves, who gave their lives over to martyrdom, who preserved the faith in the midst of great persecution, and who passed on not only that faith, but that structure of leadership, which they had received from the Apostles.

Some might say, "Oh, but you're just using the *word* overseer and giving it a meaning different from what the Apostles meant; they simply meant elders, or a group of local leaders in a local congregation." While this is no place for an extended debate about the subject[5], I would offer two simple responses. First, the Apostles use *another* word for the office of elders (more about that next), and second, the men ordained by the Apostles speak of the office of *episkopos* in precisely the same way I am using it. Case in point: Ignatius of Antioch. Born around the same time that

---

[5] For those who *are* interested in an extended discourse, I suggest three books in particular: Kirk, K.E. (*et al*), *The Apostolic Ministry: Essays on the History and Doctrine of Episcopacy*, London, Hodder & Staughton, 1962; Lightfoot, J.B., *St. Paul's Epistle to the Philippians*, Peabody, MA, Hedrickson, 1993 (originally published in 1868), of particular interested is the dissertation *The Christian Ministry*, pp. 181-269; Staley, Vernon, *The Catholic Religion*, Harrisburg, PA, Morehouse, 1983 (originally published in 1893), of particular interest are chapters 3 and 4.

Paul was converted (c. A.D. 35), and dying a
martyr shortly after the turn of the first
century (fed to lions in Rome), Ignatius was
appointed by Peter himself as the Bishop of
Antioch. After his arrest, while on his way to
Rome under lock and key (not unlike Saint
Paul before him), Ignatius penned letters to
the bishops, clergy and congregations in each
town along the path of his journey. In these
letters he wrote with clarity about the
sacrament of Holy Communion and about the
office of the bishop. To offer just one of many
examples, Ignatius wrote to the Church in
Ephesus - a church which had only a
generation before been founded by Paul,
which hosted for many years the beloved
Apostle John, which had as its first bishop
Timothy, and was now overseen by the saintly
Onesimus (whom tradition tells us was the
same Onesimus who had once been a runaway
slave, but later a servant to Paul, and about
whom the epistle to Philemon was written),

> Therefore it is fitting for you to run
> your race together with the bishop's
> purpose - as you do. For your
> presbytery [*body of elders; priests*] -
> worthy of fame, worthy of God - is
> attuned to the bishop like strings to a
> lyre. Therefore by your unity and
> harmonious love Jesus Christ is sung.

Each of you must be part of this chorus so that, being harmonious in unity, receiving God's pitch in unison, you may sing with one voice through Jesus Christ to the Father, so that he may both hear you and recognize you, through what you do well, as members of his Son. Therefore it is profitable for you to be in blameless unison, so that you may always participate in God.[6]

Bishops, returning to our metaphor, are the directors of the Church. And they are the directors of the worship of the Church. It is the responsibility of the bishops to guard the faith, doctrine and worship of the Church as these have been received from the Apostles. Typically, and throughout the history of the Church, although bishops have the particular care of a single local congregation, they also oversee a group of churches, called a diocese, which is usually, but not always, geographically based.

The liturgy - the script of the play - belongs to the whole Church, but is the particular property of the bishops, who have

----

[6] Ignatius' Epistle to the Ephesians, Chapter 4; Sparks, Jack N., *The Apostolic Fathers*, Minneapolis, Light and Life Publishers, 1978, p. 78f.

the responsibility to direct the clergy and congregations in their worship of God. The bishop's directing - his influence - will be seen in the drama of worship just like a great theater or movie director leaves his mark on the drama. But no theatrical director can simply completely rewrite the drama and still call it Shakespeare, and a truly great director is almost unnoticed because the attention is on the drama itself. In the same way, bishops have a responsibility, not to creatively rework the liturgy, but to portray it faithfully, in keeping with what has been delivered down to them from the time of the Apostles onward.

Priests   The office of priest emerged almost immediately in the life of the early Church. Not unlike the "ruler of the synagogue" in the Jewish religion of Jesus' time, Christian priests are the leaders of the local congregations of the Church. When the persecution against Christians began in Jerusalem (cf. Acts 7) two things happened: Christians were dispersed throughout Judea and Samaria and other countries, and the Apostles also were dispersed and began their missionary efforts in other regions. The need soon emerged for representatives of the Apostles (and the bishops who succeeded them) to lead local congregations throughout the world. The book of James, one of the first books of the New Testament to be written[7], is a pastoral document - a kind of pastor's manual - from James, the bishop of Jerusalem, to the priests ("brothers") who had scattered from Jerusalem after the first great persecution.

And so, almost immediately after the Day of Pentecost (Acts 2), the structure emerged of (1) Apostles doing the missionary work of establishing the Church, (2) Bishops overseeing several congregations (*a la* James in Jerusalem, who was not, by the way, one of the Twelve Apostles), and (3) priests overseeing local congregations under the direction of their bishop.

The word priest (*presbyteros* in Greek, which became *presbyter* in Latin, then *prestre* in Old French, then *prester* in Middle English and finally *priest* in modern English) literally means *elder* or *mature one*, and refers to those men who are chosen to lead God's flock because of their maturity in spiritual matters and in God's Word. In the Apostolic Church the office of elder was an ordained office for

---

[7] For a convincing argument that the Epistle of James was in fact the very first book of the New Testament to be written, and for an insightful commentary on the entire epistle, cf. Scaer, David P., *James: The Apostle of Faith*, London, Wipf & Stock Publishers, 2004.

life, and not an elected office of a congregational representative as is often found in churches today. One of the Apostles' jobs in establishing the Church was the appointing of priests or elders for the congregations: "Paul and Barnabas appointed [*ordained*] *elders* for them in each church and, with prayer and fasting, committed them to the Lord, in whom they had put their trust" (Acts 14.23). When the Apostle Paul sent Bishop Titus to Crete, he wrote, "The reason I left you in Crete was that you might straighten out what was left unfinished and appoint [*ordain*] *elders* in every town, as I directed you" (Titus 1.5). Later, the aged Apostle Peter would write to the congregations under his care, "To the *elders* among you, I appeal as a fellow *elder*, a witness to Christ's sufferings and one who also will share in the glory to be revealed: Be shepherds of God's flock that is under your care, serving as overseers - not because you must, but because you are willing, as God wants you to be..." (1 Peter 5.1f).

The priest's duties include caring for the local congregation, celebrating the sacraments, and teaching and preaching God's word, under the direction of the bishop. He is, using the analogy of theater, a leading man in the drama of worship.

Deacons The final office of leadership finds its birth in Acts 6, when seven men were chosen to be servants on behalf of the Apostles to the Church. A situation arose in the earliest days of the Church when widows needed caring for, and things were being mishandled because of a lack of organization. Finally the Apostles ordained seven men, chosen from among the congregation in Jerusalem, to "wait tables" and care for the widows in their need. The office was originally designed to free the Apostles from the daily cares of the congregation, so they could spend time in prayer and study. Taking the name of the office from the Greek word for servant (*diakonos*), these men were called deacons.

Later, Paul would include them when he wrote and spoke of the leadership of the Church: "Paul and Timothy, servants of Christ Jesus, To all the saints in Christ Jesus in Philippi, together with the overseers and *deacons*..." To Bishop Timothy, the Apostle wrote, "*Deacons*, likewise, are to be men worthy of respect, sincere, not indulging in much wine, and not pursuing dishonest gain..." (1 Timothy 3.8).

In much of the modern Protestant Church the role of deacon is that of a lay representative elected by the congregation to serve a few years in the church's leadership - usually hiring or firing the pastor. In the biblical and historic model, deacons are the hands, eyes, and ears of the bishop, ministering on his behalf to the church, and honored to serve, not only at the table of the widows, but at the Table of the Lord. The deacon's stole, worn across his shoulder and tied at the waist, is a symbol of the servant's towel. Going back to the analogy of theater, the deacon might be seen as not only an actor in the drama of redemption, but also as an important stage-hand, making sure everything is ready and in order, so the people of God can offer the sacrifice of thanksgiving.

There are other ministries in the Church, there are other roles and offices, but these are the three *ordained* offices. The bishops, priests and deacons serve as a kind of skeleton or framework on which the rest of the Church's ministry is built. Together with this leadership, the entire people of God work in unity to bring about the witness, work and worship of the Church of God.

Chapter Five

I Love To Tell The Story:
God's Word For God's People

Have you heard the story about the man who lost his will to live and planned to commit suicide, only to be interrupted by an angel named Clarence and then shown what the world would have been like without him? Or how about this - have you heard the tragic tale of the young couple desperately in love, but because their families were enemies, couldn't find a way to be together? Toward the end, she takes a potion that makes it *look* like she's dead, but he thinks she really is dead, so he poisons himself. When she awakens she is heartbroken, so she pierces her own heart with a dagger.

Most likely you know the tales well. The first is *It's A Wonderful Life*, the classic movie directed by Frank Capra and starring Jimmy Stewart. The second is, obviously, *Romeo and Juliet*, the star-crossed lovers' tale by William Shakespeare. What you may not have known is that the Capra movie is based on *The Greatest Gift*, a short story by Philip Van Doren Stern. And Shakespeare took his tale from an older story as well - actually two: Ovid's *Pyramus and Thisbe*, and Xenophon's *Ephesiaca*.

Good dramas are based on good stories. The drama of Christian worship is based on the greatest story of all - the story of the creation and redemption of the world by God through Jesus Christ. If what we do in worship is a play, the play is based on a story - and the story is found in Holy Scripture. The Bible is the basis for our worship, and it is the story of the Bible which we dramatize every time we gather together to worship.

"He Will Guide You Into All Truth"

When Jesus inaugurated the Reign of God and established the Church as the people of that Reign, he did not abandon them to simply fend for themselves in a hostile world.

He promised to send the Holy Spirit as a teacher and guide for them in their new work. On the Day of Pentecost, when the Holy Spirit was given, he wasn't making a one-time cameo appearance. He came to stay. The promise recorded in John 16.13, "But when he, the Spirit of truth, comes, he will guide you into all truth," is a continuing promise of God to the Church.

Having said that, we should realize that the Holy Spirit *did* guide the Apostles into all truth as he inspired them to write Holy Scriptures (just as he had inspired the Old Testament writers before them). These Scriptures serve the Church as the *primary* measure of truth. Consider this sampling of the witness of the centuries:

Saint Caesarius of Arles: The sacred Scriptures have been transmitted to us like letters from our heavenly country.[8]

Saint Thomas Aquinas: [The Church] uses the authority of canonical Scriptures as an incontrovertible proof, and the authority of the doctors of the

---

[8] Mueller, Mary Magdalene, translator; *The Fathers of the Church: St. Caesarius; Sermons, Volume 1*; Washington, DC; Catholic University Press of America 1956; Sermon 7, p. 46.

Church as one that may properly be used, yet merely as probable. For our faith rests upon the revelation made to the apostles and prophets, who wrote the canonical books, and not on the revelations (if any such there are) made to other doctors.[9]

The Articles of Religion of the Church of England: Holy Scripture containeth all things necessary to salvation; so that whatsoever is not read therein, nor may be proved thereby, is not to be required of any man, that it should be believed as an article of the Faith, or be thought requisite or necessary to salvation.[10]

These are only a few statements representing an idea which saturates the writings of the Church and declares the Scriptures to have *the most prominent place of authority* in the life of the Church and the lives of believers. Lest this be thought a sectarian teaching, it should be noted that this is the express teaching of the ancient undivided

---

[9] Thomas Aquinas, *Summa Theologica*, 1.1.8, in Kreeft, Peter, *Summa of the Summa*, San Francisco, Ignatius Press, 1990, p. 47.

[10] Article 26.

Church, and of the later Catholic, Orthodox and Protestant streams.

What Is The Bible?

Perhaps the best place to start in defining the Bible is to define three important words related to it.

Bible   The word Bible itself is from the Greek *biblia*, which means a collection of books or writings. *Biblia* means a portfolio. The Christian portfolio of Scriptures - the Christian *biblia* or Bible, is that set of writings recognized as the inspired Word of God.

Inspiration The word inspiration comes from the Latin *in spire*, meaning to breathe into. Inspiration is the act by which God directed the writers of the Holy Scriptures. He "breathed into" their writings, guiding them according to his will, so that their words were at once human, and at the same time divine (it is worth noting that in Hebrew, Greek and Latin, the word for *breath* is the same as the word for *Spirit*: *ruach, pneuma* and *spire* [*spiritu*]).

Canon   The final word of importance for understanding what the Bible is is the word canon, from the Greek *canon* which means an *official list*. We get our English word *cane* from the same root, the idea being that a cane serves as a measuring *rod*, a yard*stick*; the canon, then, is our yardstick of authorized books. If Bible means "collection of books", and inspiration speaks to the process of those books being written, the word canon simply means those books which are officially recognized by the Church as inspired, as part of the collection.[11]

Our Bible, our collection of books recognized as inspired by God, has two parts. The first part, the *Old Testament*, is the story of God and man from the creation of the world to just before the birth of Jesus, when God became man and joined heaven and earth. The Old Testament includes the Law (the first five books, written by Moses), the Prophets (including the historical section and the writings of the prophets themselves) and the Wisdom books (the Psalms, Proverbs and other poetry and prose).

---

[11] A technical distinction important to note: the canon *could* contain a book not inspired, and likewise an inspired book *could* have been left out of the canon. It is the faith of the Church that the same Spirit which guided the Apostles in the writing of the texts, later guided their successors in the gathering and canonization of the texts.

The second part, the *New Testament*, is the story of God and man from the birth of Jesus Christ to the establishment of the Church in the first century. The New Testament includes, in something of a correlation to the Old, the Gospels (the first four books, which tell the story of Jesus), the History (the book of Acts), and the Epistles (the letters of the Apostles and the book of the Revelation).

The focus of the Bible - from beginning to end, from Genesis to Revelation, both the Old and the New Testaments - is God's creation of the world, its fall, and his redemption of it through Jesus Christ. The two "halves" make a seamless whole. It has been said of the two testaments, "The New is in the Old contained; the Old is in the New explained." Both serve to point to Christ. Both tell the greatest story ever told.

More About Inspiration

Inspiration, as we have already seen, is the act of God breathing into the writings of the Apostles and others, so that their words became not only their own, but also God's. When we say that Scripture is inspired we are saying that those pages contain more than the mere wisdom of human beings (however good and wise they may have been). We are saying that the words of the Bible transcend all other writings, and are in fact the *revelation* of God to his people.

Today a significant number of people who call themselves Christians don't believe in the authority and inspiration of the Bible, and consider those who do to be somewhat backward and uneducated. While, on the one hand, they elevate Jesus Christ as the epitome of wisdom (even if they may not be ready to acknowledge him as God come in the flesh), on the other hand they completely dismiss *his own* understanding of the authority of Scripture. They are, in short, making themselves wiser than God.

Jesus was a man of the Word. In the Gospels he referenced the Old Testament (which would have been his "Bible") more than a hundred and fifty times. He considered the voice of Scripture to be the voice of God. Read *carefully* these words from Jesus: "'Haven't you read,' he replied, 'that at the beginning the Creator 'made them male and female and said "For this reason a man will leave his father and mother and be united to his wife..."'" (Matthew 19.4f). Did you see it? Do you want to read it one more time before I show you what Jesus just did?

Jesus quoted Genesis 2, and *attributed to the voice of God a comment made by the author.* If you go back and look at Genesis 2, the text doesn't say, "God said, 'For this reason a man will leave his father and his mother...'" In the Genesis text, God doesn't say it, Moses says it. When Jesus attributes it to God, he is recognizing the whole of Scripture as being the voice of God. "So truly is God regarded as the author of scriptural statements that in certain contexts 'God' and 'Scripture' have become interchangeable."[12]

In another place, Jesus considers the writings of David to actually be the voice of the Holy Spirit: "How is it then that David, *speaking by the Spirit*, calls him 'Lord'?" (Matthew 22.43). Jesus understood Scriptures to be the source of truth and life. He accused his opposition of being in error because they did "not know the Scriptures or the power of God" (Mark 12.24).

The Apostles, trained by Christ and continuing his work, held Holy Scripture in the same high regard. They understood the

---

[12] John Wenham; cited in Johnson, Alan & Webber, Robert, *What Christians Believe: A Biblical and Historical Summary* Grand Rapids, MI, Zondervan, 1989, p. 23.

Scriptures to be Spirit-inspired, just as Jesus did. Paul wrote, *"All Scripture is God-breathed* and is useful for teaching, rebuking, correcting and training in righteousness, so that the man of God may be thoroughly equipped for every good work"* (2 Timothy 3.16f), and Peter wrote, "Above all, you must understand that no prophecy of Scripture came about by the prophet's own interpretation. For prophecy never had its origin in the will of man, but *men spoke from God* as they were *carried along by the Holy Spirit"* (2 Peter 1.20). Ironic, isn't it, and logically fallacious, that some modern people call themselves followers of Christ, and yet follow neither him nor his disciples in their high regard for the Bible as the very Word of God?

The Bible And The Church

"Well, isn't it wonderful that *I* have the Word of God now, and *I* can hear God for myself?" Some well-meaning and devout Christians who would not dare even consider a liberal position that makes the Scriptures anything less than the very Word of God make a similar mistake in thinking of the Bible as the word of God spoken *directly* to them as individuals.

I have a priest friend who made the point better than I can:

A few years back, I had an interesting conversation with a friend who believed he could study and understand the Bible without the aid of the Church. We were close so I felt comfortable asking him, "Whom do you worship on Sunday?"

"Christ," he said.

Then I gently probed, "Which Christ? The Eutychian, Gnostic, Docetic, Arian, Nestorian, or Ebionite Christ?"

His smile told me he understood.

Those who read and interpret the Bible apart from the Church are on tenuous ground. False teachers have always appealed to the Bible alone to support their beliefs. The Jehovah's Witnesses for example have some convincing exegesis to verify that their "Christ" is the Christ of Bible. But the one thing heretics cannot do is appeal to the historic witness of the Church to support their beliefs.[13]

The Bible cannot be separated from the Church, nor the Church from the Bible. The Bible is the Church's book. The Church wrote it (the Apostles were, after all, members - founders - of the Church), the Church canonized it, and the Church interprets it.

In the 19th Century, the radically independent Alexander Campbell, founder of the Church of Christ movement, advised that he did and we should "open the New Testament as if mortal man had never seen it before." I hope you see the fatal flaw in that thinking! To even "open" the New Testament is to recognize that mortal men have seen it before. Where did it come from? Who gathered the twenty seven books into one? Who says these and not others constitute the New Testament? It is *impossible* to read it "as if mortal man had never seen it before," and to do so is not only silly, it is also rebellious. It is, as Robert Wilken said, a kind of "self imposed

[13] Fr. Doug Sangster, *Clarifying Sola Scriptura*, http://holytrinityrec.org/AFAC/?p=26

amnesia."[14] Instead, we recognize that the Scriptures are properly interpreted and understood only in the context of the People of God. "We know the true meaning of the Bible by the general consent of the Church, influenced by the indwelling presence of the Holy Spirit."[15]

The Book of Acts tells the story of an Ethiopian eunuch who had been to Jerusalem in search of God. On his way home he was in his chariot reading the Scriptures, but he couldn't understand it for himself. He needed the help of the Church. "Then Philip ran up to the chariot and heard the man reading Isaiah the prophet. 'Do you understand what you are reading?' Philip asked. 'How can I,' he said, 'unless someone explains it to me?' So he invited Philip to come up and sit with him" (Acts 8.30f).

For those who insist that they need the Scriptures and nothing or no one else in order to hear God, I will let Scripture itself address the matter. The Apostle Paul wrote to

---

[14] Hall, Christopher A., *Reading Scripture with the Church Fathers*, Downers Grove, IL, InterVarsity Press, 1998, p. 14ff.

[15] Staley, Vernon, *The Catholic Religion*, Harrisburg, PA, Morehouse, 1983 (originally published 1893), p. 200f.

Timothy, "Although I hope to come to you soon, I am writing you these instructions so that, if I am delayed, you will know how people ought to conduct themselves in God's household, which is the church of the Living God, *the pillar and foundation of truth*" (1 Timothy 3.14f). The Bible is the Word of God, and the Church is the pillar and foundation of truth. The two go hand in hand.

Chapter Six

It Didn't Just
Fall From The Sky:
How We Got The Bible

Good scripts are not just for the stage. They are also read as literature. Most likely you didn't first encounter *Hamlet* by attending the Globe Theater in London, or any other theater for that matter. Chances are your first exposure to *Hamlet* came by *reading* it - probably in a classroom, and, depending on how good your teacher was, possibly bored out of your mind with the whole enterprise.

Hamlet, like other great literature, doesn't just "happen." In a recent poll of literature teachers around the world the novel *Don Quixote* by Miguel Cervantes was voted "the greatest novel of all time." I read it for the first time when I was in my forties (yes, I know, I'm a late bloomer), and I was mesmerized. I laughed out loud at practically every page. I couldn't put it down. I stayed up late into the night reading it. My wife finally banished me from the bedroom because my laughter was keeping her awake. But think with me, for a moment, about how *Don Quixote* made it into my hands. First, it was written by Miguel Cervantes in 1605, and when I say written, I mean *handwritten*! In Spain. In Spanish. The original title is *El Ingenioso Hidalgo Don Quixote De La Mancha*. After being written, it was typeset, each letter of the book being hand set on primitive printing plates. Then it was printed. Reprinted. And reprinted again. Eventually it was translated into English (the best translation being by Edith Grossman at the late date of 2003). Then it was printed on high-tech modern printers. Then it was shipped to warehouses and bookstores. Then I bought a copy and read it. Then I took it with me on a trip to Spain and had my photo taken rereading it beneath the famous windmills of La Mancha. OK. Enough already! My point is that Miguel Cervantes didn't write it directly for me. There was a very long and complicated 400 year process of getting it from his pen into my hands.

In the same way, the script of our play - the story on which our drama of worship is based- didn't just fall down out of the sky all leather-bound and red-lettered. Devout Christians properly place a great emphasis on the inspiration of the Bible and recognize it as the source of authority in the Church; they have made great stands for the Bible's uniqueness, its infallibility, and its primacy. But few have taken time to consider its origin, and the process by which it came to us. Some imagine a scenario something like this: Paul wrote the letters, saved a copy of them to his files, gave them to Luke, who gathered them with the writings of the other Apostles, and *presto!*, there was the New Testament in all its glory. Some people assume that the Apostles themselves flipped through the pages of the first edition of the New Testament, remarking about what a fine production it was!

Upon any reflection at all, it becomes obvious that the New Testament didn't come to us in that fashion. The problem really isn't that people have thought incorrectly about the process which brought us the Bible, but that people haven't thought much about it at all.

The Old Testament Canon

The Old Testament canon began with the writings of Moses, the first five books of the Bible, written about 1200 B.C. Succeeding generations of the Jewish people added to the canon with books recounting the history of Israel, the ministry of the prophets, and the wisdom and poetry of David, Solomon and others.

In the fourth century before the birth of Christ a great dispersion occurred in Israel, with the Hebrew people traveling, trading, and relocating, literally throughout the known world (by the time of Jesus there were Jewish colonies as far away as modern-day England). This dispersion created two different groups of Jews: the Palestinian Jews who remained in the homeland and spoke Hebrew or Aramaic, and the Jews of the Diaspora (meaning *scattering*) who had relocated throughout the world and spoke the global language of Greek.

In about 300 B.C. a group of Jewish scholars met in Alexandria, Egypt and began translating the Old Testament into Greek - the first time the canon had been translated out of

Hebrew into another language.[16] This version
of Scripture is to this day called the *Septuagint*,
(meaning *seventy*) - from the number of
scholars involved in the translation.

Whereas the Jews in the homeland had
a canon that stopped around 400 B.C. (i.e.,
with Malachi), the Greek canon included
books that covered the history of God's people
for the next 400 years, up to just before the
birth of Christ. These "extra" books are called
the Deuterocanonical books.[17]

The Deuterocanonical Books

The Deuterocanonical (*second canon*)
books are the books contained in the Greek
Old Testament, but not in the Palestinian
canon. As an historical note, the Palestinian
canon did not become "official" until the
Pharisees' Council of Jamnia, around A.D. 90.
This council was held twenty years after the
destruction of Jerusalem in A.D. 70, and was
composed of Pharisees seeking to rebuild
Judaism without a Temple or sacrifices. The
Pharisees looked at the Greek additions as

---

[16] The work of translation continued until 132 B.C.

[17] For a good study of the process of canonization, cf.
Pelikan, Jaroslav, *Whose Bible Is It?*, New York, Viking,
2005.

impure, in that they did not come from Israel, and excluded them from their canon. At the same time, early Christians were already appealing to these very texts in the defense of Christian doctrine.

Among Christians, the Old Testament books were simply "received", and the early Church used the Greek canon in its study, apologetics and worship. Having said that, there was never an ecumenical council of the Church which officially determined the exact Old Testament canon.[18]

The New Testament Canon

Although the books of the New Testament were all written before the

---

[18] Among the various branches of the Christian Church there are different approaches to the Old Testament. The Roman Catholic and Eastern Orthodox Churches accept the full Greek Canon. The Anglican Church accepts the Deuterocanonical books "as Saint Jerome sayeth, 'for edification of the people, but not for the proving of the doctrines of the Church'" (Article Six, Articles of Religion). The Protestant Churches accept only the Palestinian canon, but have some of their brightest lights calling for a broader canon (cf. F.F. Bruce, *The Canon of Scripture*, Downers Grove, IL, InterVarsity Press, 1988).

destruction of Jerusalem in A.D. 70[19] (the year Jerusalem was destroyed by the Roman army, as prophesied by Jesus in Matthew 24, Mark 13 and Luke 21), these books were not gathered into a final canon until the fourth century A.D.

There are five important steps in the progression of the New Testament Canon:

The Christ Event The life of Jesus serves as a completion and fulfillment of the Old Testament, and was the source of the New Testament.

The Apostolic Writings As the Apostles taught, they also wrote, and their memoirs and letters began to circulate in the young Church, and were received as authoritative.

The Canon of Marcion The first written list of the New Testament books was made by a heretic. Marcion was the son of a bishop in Asia Minor who, in about the year 150, began his own religion, after being

---

[19] The debate among scholars has raged for centuries, but for a convincing summary of the early date argument, cf. Gentry, Kenneth, *Before Jerusalem Fell: Dating the Book of Revelation*; Atlanta, GA, American Vision, 1999.

excommunicated by his own father for seducing a young virgin. He taught that Jesus was a different god from the Old Testament god Jehovah, and he created his own canon including only the passages he liked! He completely rejected the Old Testament (it was, after all, about a different god!), and he excised any apostolic writings that quoted the Old Testament or referred to it favorably. This left him with a very edited version of the Gospel of Luke, and significantly reduced epistles of Paul.[20]

What was significant about Marcion's canon is that it forced the early Church to begin dealing with the question of what was and wasn't Scripture. As a rule, *heresy precedes orthodoxy*. Things flow along nicely until someone begins some silly false teaching; then the Church has to address the matter and firmly declare its own position.

The Gnostic Invasion The Gnostics were a cult which claimed to have *special* knowledge about Christ and salvation which had been *secretly* passed down to them from

---

[20] Interestingly, centuries later Thomas Jefferson would do much the same thing, literally cutting and pasting his own version of the New Testament with the miracles of Jesus excised.

the Apostles. Their "secret" teaching amounted to a mixture of paganism and Christian thought, with the person of Jesus Christ diminished (not unlike the modern New Age movement). The Church's argument agains Gnosticism was threefold:

First, the Church stated that the Apostolic Tradition was authoritative.

Second, it said the Apostolic Tradition was available to all (and not secretly hidden) in the writings of the Apostles.

Third, the Church declared that the Apostolic Tradition was guarded through bishops chosen by the Apostles, and that the continuity of those bishops was guarded by Apostolic Succession.

These bishops - the true and legitimate heirs of the Apostles - began to make lists of books to be recognized as Scripture in their dioceses. These early lists might be created by a single bishop, or by several bishops in conference, and the lists vary slightly according to the bishops' own knowledge.

The first bishop to give us the exact list we now recognize as the New Testament was Saint Athanasius, the bishop of Alexandria,

Egypt (who had earlier, as a deacon, boldly defended the faith at the Council of Nicea in 325, and who led in the crafting of the Nicene Creed). In his Easter Letter of 367, written to the priests and congregations throughout Egypt, he enumerated the twenty seven books we now receive as the New Testament.

The Council of Carthage   In 397, thirty years after Athanasius' letter, and more than 350 years after the birth of the Church on the Day of Pentecost, a group of bishops, priests and deacons met in Carthage (modern day Tunis, Tunisia) for a regional council which prescribed the limits of the canon as the same set forth by Athanasius.

After Carthage other councils throughout the world recognized the same books as constituting the New Testament, so that by the middle of the 5th Century the canon was universally established. It must be said again: the process of canonization did not make the Scriptures inspired; the Holy Spirit inspired them as they were written by the Apostles. In the long process of canonization, the Church - led by the same Holy Spirit - simply recognized those particular writings as the inspired Word of God.

The Bible is the Church's book! It was written by the founders. It was gathered by the early leaders. It was set apart by the councils. And it has been the source of life and truth for every generation in the Church. How shall we respond to so great a gift as God's Word?

Chapter Seven

Scripture As Script:
How To Use The Bible

James Spader, the Boston-born actor of television and movies, has a photographic memory. He looks at the pages of the script and memorizes them. When he is acting, he visualizes the script and simply says what he reads with his mind's eye. James Spader is a very unusual actor. Most actors spend a great deal of time with the script, familiarizing themselves with the lines and the stage notes, long before stepping onto the stage or in front of the camera.

Many Christians, on the other hand, enter into the act of worship "cold turkey," not having familiarized themselves with the script at all. They go to the worship service seeing themselves not as actors offering the drama of thanksgiving, not even as participants in the event (except for singing a few songs and mumbling "Amen" to a few prayers - and in many modern churches even the singing and praying has become a stage show), but seeing themselves instead as spectators, observers, auditors - people who are are there to look and listen and not much else. Some churches unintentionally promote this behavior because the leadership itself sees the congregation as "the audience," and at best the scriptural focus for any given Sunday is whatever short text the pastor decides to preach on - oftentimes not chosen until the night before!

Liturgical churches, which have the benefit of an ordered lectionary, have the advantage of knowing ahead of time what the Scripture readings will be for the service - and they have the advantage of having lots of Scripture to read - usually an Old Testament lesson, a Psalm, a lesson from an Epistle, and a reading from the Gospels (thereby making liturgical churches more Word-centered than churches which label themselves Word Churches). Still, many if not most Christians who worship in a liturgical church don't take the time to prepare for the service. Like their non-liturgical brothers and sisters, they tend to think of themselves as auditors ("I wonder what I'm going to *hear* this morning?") rather than actors ("I'm ready for my role this morning!").

It is a sad thing that, holding in their hands this amazing script - inspired by the Holy Spirit, written by the Apostles, collected by the early Church, preserved for nearly 2000 years - many Christians nonchalantly disregard it except with the briefest of attention. But until the Scriptures are *used*, they have not accomplished the purpose for which they were given by God. The Bible was given, not simply as the story of God's people, nor as a kind of rule book to which we refer every now and then, but as the source of continual life and insight. The Holy Spirit inspired their writing, collection and preservation, and the same Holy Spirit uses them to train, comfort, direct and encourage His people now, and to reveal to them God's truth and wisdom. In short, God *continues* to speak to his Church through his Word.

Reading The Script

If you find yourself belonging to that company of believers who haven't made the Scriptures a real part of life, what follows are some practical suggestions for reading the

Bible. The recommendations which follow are very personal - they are things you can do alone, at home, or in the company of a small group - but it should be clear by now that the *primary* use of the Word of God is in the context of the whole Church - our gathering together for worship, and our living together as the People of God.

The beginning place when approaching the Bible is to simply read it. Pick it up, and start reading it. We should not, however, approach it as some kind of crystal ball; that is, we should not randomly open it, read where our eyes may fall, and assume that we are doing any kind of justice to understanding the script. No actor approaches his lines this way; no one reads a novel or a textbook or a biography like this. Why then, when we come to the most important and powerful book in history, do we think of it as a kind of magic eight ball which we shake for an answer to our questions? When you read the Bible...

Read Often The Scriptures should be read, not legalistically, but faithfully. This means daily, or at least several times a week, but the point is saturation. The more the believer immerses himself in the Word of God, the more the Word of God forms his life.

Read Prayerfully Christians, who have the Holy Spirit residing within them, should approach the Scriptures with the anticipation of hearing God. At its best, Bible reading is a conversation with God - he speaks to us and we speak to him.

Read Intentionally Sometimes faithful and devout Christians hurry through the daily readings in order to "get it done." Once finished, they have done their duty, but without thinking for a moment about what they read. The Bible should be approached intentionally, with the anticipation of encountering truth. Better a little, contemplated, than a lot, skimmed.

Read Methodically The Sunday lectionary used in liturgical churches affords the reader a program to follow. There are also daily lectionaries, and other Bible reading plans; but whatever you use, involve yourself in a good program of reading instead of just randomly opening the Bible and reading wherever the pages fall. I also suggest that a good program of reading is not just a straight-through run from Genesis to Revelation; rather it will offer on a daily basis portions from the various parts of the Bible - not unlike a meal of meat, vegetables, bread and dessert.

Studying The Bible

Great actors not only read the script, they study it. They get in character; they interview people; the visit places. Reading the Bible may be likened to everyday meals, but studying the Bible is more like preparing, cooking and serving a gourmet feast. Unlike regular daily reading, which covers a "healthy portion" of Scriptures week in and week out, in-depth study may focus on one passage or even one verse for a lengthy period of time. You may take an entire afternoon just looking up what the words of a verse mean, and how they are used elsewhere in the Bible. Studying the Bible means savoring it - working the bone - tasting every bit of the flavor. Studying, like cooking a gourmet meal, involves a threefold process of preparation (getting the materials together for study - dictionaries, commentaries, etc.), cooking (the actual work of attentive study), and serving and eating (applying the truths we have discovered to our own lives, and sharing them with others).

I suggest a fourfold process for studying God's Word:

Prayer Begin with an attitude of prayer and openness, anticipating that God is going to reveal truths and applications to you which you have not seen before.

Exegesis   Using the Bible and the study tools, learn what the text *means*. Learn what the words mean in their original language (it's not hard to do in the computer age). What did the writer mean when he first wrote it? What was the historical context? Too often, people assume they are studying the Bible when they read it a bit, think about it a bit, and then apply it to themselves. But they have completely missed this vital step of "getting out of" (*exegesis*) the text what it really means.

Interpretation   Having learned the meaning of the text, now is the time to interpret it. This is the moment of understanding the "original intent" of the text. Ask the question, "How did this apply to the situation of the first readers?" It is not only helpful, but also essential, to listen to what others say when it comes to this process of interpretation. We do not approach the Bible as if we were the first ones to find it. We listen to what God has shown others, from modern faithful writers all the way back to the early fathers of the Church.

Application   Finally we ask, "How does this apply to me, to my family, to my church, to my situation?" Application is the process of learning which principles, gleaned from the study, can be applied to our lives. And so, study isn't done for the exercise of study alone - it is done to transform us into men and women God has called us to be.

Meditation

If simple reading is like eating a simple meal, and if studying is like preparing and enjoying a gourmet feast, then meditation might be likened to a quiet after-dinner conversation with friends around a glowing fireplace.

The human brain is divided into two halves, each behaving very differently from the other. The left side of the brain controls the right side of the body, and is also used for logic, working equations, categorizing, and processing data. The right side of the brain controls the left side of the body, and is also used for the creative skills - music, painting, imagining, intuiting. Study is a left brain function. Meditating is a right brain function.

In meditating we do not approach the Bible in order to "learn" something; instead we place ourselves in the story - we use our senses. We taste the fish and bread as Jesus feeds the 5000; we hear the gravelly voice of John the Baptist's call for repentance; we smell the incense as angels worship at God's throne; we feel the stinging wind-driven rain as the disciples cross the stormy Sea of Galilee. Meditation is not the time for study tools, but for imagination. It is a time for putting flesh onto the skeleton of our study. *Meditation is to study as storytelling is to teaching*; it brings it alive. And it is also crazy dangerous!

I know a minister who was really into meditation. He had even written books on it. He traveled the country lecturing on it. Then one day, in his meditation, he thought he heard God tell him to divorce his wife and take up with another woman. Everyone told him he had missed God but this man shunned them all. He had put his meditation above the authority of all else, including his pastor and the commonsense faith of the Church. He divorced his wife, ran off with another woman, severely damaged his family and destroyed his ministry. Meditation, unchecked, is devastation. Like nuclear energy, it can be used for wonderful good or for destructive evil. Here, then, are a few guidelines for meditation.

Meditation Follows Study Don't start meditating as your first act of approaching the Scriptures. Read the text first, then study the text, *then* meditate on the text. Don't get the cart before the horse.

Begin With A Story The Epistles tend to be full of concepts while the Gospels are full of stories. I suggest you choose a story from the life of Christ and put yourself in it.

Use The Story As A Guide With the studied story marking out the boundaries of the meditation, watch the life of the story unfold. Put yourself into it. Notice every detail. Close your eyes. Savor the moment.

Listen For God Meditation is not just an exercise in imagination; it is a means of listening to the living voice of the Holy Spirit. Allow God to speak to you through your meditation, applying what you hear and learn to your life.

Submit To Others Finally, always submit your meditation to the more objective tools of reading and study, and if your meditation leads you to any significant applications or decisions, *always* submit it to the wisdom of those who have spiritual authority in your life, as well as to the wisdom of the whole Church from ages past to now.

What we do as actors in the great story of salvation is this: we hear, proclaim, reenact and celebrate the Word of God. We come into His presence declaring his truth. We add our thanks to the Scriptures being read. We come to his Table because the Bible commends it. We go out into the world proclaiming his Good News. Every part of the drama of redemption is saturated in the Word of God. It is the script of our worship, and of our lives.

Chapter Eight

Mimicking The Masters:
Why Worship Should Be Liturgical

If someone asks you to get together with them and put on a production of *Little Orphan Annie*, and then tells you, "We're not really going to use a script, and we'll just kind of figure it out as we go along," you would think them mad. If they told you it wasn't going to be a story about a little orphaned girl who comes into the life of the wealthy Daddy Warbucks, but instead was just going to be a couple of songs from the musical, and no storyline, you might say to them, "Well, all right, but that *isn't Little Orphan Annie*!" Standard plays have standard scripts and standard storylines. Even when someone reworks a Shakespearian play into a modern setting, the *story* is still the same! Why, then, do we think it is no problem to just throw together whatever we choose, and call it the worship of God? In the Bible, from the beginning to the end, the worship of God was the most important thing in the life of the People of God, and therefore was *carefully* attended to. It was *cultivated* (the word *cultivate* has as its root *cult*. Today *cult* implies an aberrant religion, but its true and original meaning is "form of worship," from the Latin, *cultus*, "to care for").

Worship isn't something done haphazardly, or according to whatever will draw a crowd. This is upside down thinking, slipping back into the notion that the congregation is the audience, and the whole Sunday worship event is for them. If we see the congregation as actors on the stage, offering God the sacrifice of praise, then the question to be answered is not, "What will the people like?," but "What does God call for?"

Going a step further, great artists - be they musicians, sculptors, painters or actors - become great, not by doing their own thing, but copying the masters. Certainly there is room for an artist to be unique, to stand out above the rest, to do his art well; but these men and women didn't learn their craft in a vacuum. They schooled under those who had gone before them, they watched other great artists and learned from them, they practiced and refined their crafts. Whether we're talking about El Greco studying painting under Titian, or Al Pacino studying acting under Lee Strasberg, the greats became great by copying the greats.

Worship is the same. In our modern era of deconstructionism, when individualism is all the rage and innovation is king, we would do well to remember that it is our pleasure to please God, and all this is for him. How, then, was God worshiped by the greats who went before us?

Old Testament Worship

Adam was a priest and the garden was a Temple. It would take a whole book to explore it, and someone has already written a good one, so we'll leave it at that.[21] From creation forward God has been worshiped in an ordered way. Melchizedeck, a "priest of God Most High" served Abraham bread and wine after Abraham brought his tithe in

---

[21] Fesko, J.V., Last Things First: *Unlocking Genesis 1-3 with the Christ of Eschatology*, Glasgow, Christian Focus Publications, 2007; see also Walton, John H., *The Lost World of Genesis One: Ancient Cosmology and the Origins Debate*, Downers Grove, IL, InterVarsity Press, 2009.

thanksgiving for victory in a battle (Genesis 14.17ff).

When Moses brought the Children of Israel out of Egypt and received the Ten Commandments from God, he also received very explicit and particular instructions on every aspect of worship - from the construction of the place of worship (the Tabernacle), to the vestments of the clergy (Aaron and the Levites), to instructions regarding the sacrifices. He was even given a detailed recipe for incense and holy oil that was to be used *only* in the worship of God. Throughout the rest of the Old Testament, from David to Solomon to Ezekiel to Judas Maccabeus, every incident of worship happened in the context of liturgy and sacrifice. No one can argue that Old Testament worship wasn't liturgical and ordered. And ordered by God!

New Testament Worship

Obviously, with Jesus and the Apostles being in the milieu of Jewish worship, they too found themselves worshiping God in "the old ways," and liturgically. The early Church, while it was still umbilically connected to Judaism, continued "daily in the Temple" (Acts 2.46), doing what Jews did, praying the prayers and observing the feasts - but not the sin sacrifices (Hebrews 10.18).

"Yes, but once the Church really got rolling, that liturgy stuff was left behind," exclaim some Christians, "the Spirit-filled Church wasn't liturgical! We can't allow liturgy to quench the leading of the Spirit." Oh *really*?

In Acts 2.42, *after* the Day of Pentecost and the giving of the Spirit, the Bible tells us that the nascent Church "continued steadfastly" in four things: The Apostles doctrine and fellowship, the prayers, and the breaking of the bread. Not, mind you, "prayers," but "*the* prayers," and not just breaking any bread, but "*the* breaking of *the* bread." Order. Ceremony. Sacraments. Liturgy.

Later in Acts (13.1ff), when Paul and Barnabas by a prophetic word from the Holy Spirit were set aside for missionary work, it happened in the context of structured, ordered worship. The NIV reads, "while they were *worshiping* the Lord and fasting." Other translations have "while they were *ministering* to the Lord..." Are you ready for some Greek? Fasten your seat belts, because this is a doozy! The Greek word here is *leitourgeo*! "While they

were doing the liturgy for the Lord..." Later,
scattered throughout Saint Paul's Epistles (not
to mention Peter's and John's), we find
references to various sacramental and
liturgical actions - things which might go
unnoticed by people unfamiliar with
structured worship, but which leap off the
pages for those who worship God in the
historic way; things like "the kiss of peace"
and "the Amen" and obviously, Holy
Communion (cf. 1 Corinthians 16.20, 14.16,
and the whole of chapter 11). If modern
Christians will take off their blinders and read
the New Testament in its context, they will
discover that the New Testament Church -
from Pentecost forward - worshiped God
liturgically and sacramentally. It only stands to
reason, seeing that they were standing in
continuity from Adam to Melchizedek to Aaron
to Jesus to the Apostles, that they would
worship God in the form they had *received* from
those who went before them.

Early Church Worship

After the death of the Apostles, the
Church continued to expand through the
ministry of those directly chosen and ordained
by them, and these men were faithful not only
to the doctrine of the Apostles, but also to
their form of worship. The earliest description

we have of a Christian worship service is from the *Didache*, also called *The Teaching of the Twelve*, a kind of pastor's manual written sometime between A.D. 70 and 100. It lines out the order of worship for the Christian Churches, and the primary acts are Word and Sacrament:

> Now about the Eucharist: This is how to give thanks: First in connection with the cup: "We thank you, our Father, for the holy vine of David, your child, which you have revealed through Jesus, your child. To you be glory forever."
>
> Then in connection with the piece [broken off the loaf]: "We thank you, our Father, for the life and knowledge which you have revealed through Jesus, your child. To you be glory forever. As this piece [of bread] was scattered over the hills and then was brought together and made one, so let your Church be brought together from the ends of the earth into your Kingdom. For yours is the glory and the power through Jesus Christ forever."

> You must not let anyone eat or drink
> of your Eucharist except those
> baptized in the Lord's name.[22]

Fifty years later, around the year 150, Justin Martyr describes Christian worship in the same way, centering around the reading and proclamation of the Word of God, and the celebration of the Lord's Supper.

> And on the day called Sunday there is a
> meeting in one place of those who live
> in cities or the country, and the
> memoirs of the apostles or the writings
> of the prophets are read as long as time
> permits. When the reader has finished,
> the president in a discourse urges and
> invites [us] to the imitation of these
> noble things. Then we all stand up
> together and offer prayers. And as said
> before, when we have finished the
> prayer, bread is brought, and wine and
> water, and the president similarly sends
> up prayers and thanksgivings to the
> best of his ability, and the congregation
> assents, saying the Amen; the
> distribution, and reception of the
> consecrated [elements] by each one,

---

[22] *Didache* 9.1-9; Richardson, Cyril C.; *Early Christian Fathers*, Volume 1, Philadelphia, Westminster Press, 1953, p. 175.

takes place and they are sent to the absent by the deacons.[23]

Then comes Hippolytus, a bishop who was something of a curmudgeon and who didn't play well with others (I'm sure you know the type). Born within fifty years of the death of Saint John, he was a stickler for observing the traditions and not changing what had been received. The liturgy we have from his writings is the earliest full liturgy on record, from about the year 200, and again it follows precisely the form already observed in Paul, the *Didache* and Justin Martyr. Remember, Hippolytus was certainly no innovator, so what we have from his pen hearkens back to the generations before him - the generation of the Apostles themselves. I give you his Eucharistic prayer in full and ask you to read it slowly and carefully. If you happen to worship God in a liturgical church in the beginning of the 21st century, it will instantly ring familiar.

To [the bishop] then the deacons shall bring the offering, and he, laying his hands upon it, with all the presbytery, shall say as the thanksgiving:

---

[23] First Apology of Justin, *ibid*, p. 287f.

The Lord be with you.

And with thy spirit.

Lift up your hearts.

We lift them up unto the Lord.

Let us give thanks to the Lord.

It is meet and right.

And then he shall proceed immediately:

We give thee thanks, O God, through
thy beloved Servant Jesus Christ,
whom at the end of time thou didst send
to us as a Saviour and Redeemer and
the Messenger of thy counsel. Who is
thy Word, inseparable from thee;
through whom thou didst make all
things and in whom thou art well
pleased. Whom thou didst send from
heaven into the womb of the Virgin,
and who, dwelling within her, was made
flesh, and was manifested as thy Son,
being born of the Holy Spirit and the
Virgin. Who, fulfilling thy will, and
winning for himself a holy people,
spread out his hands when he came to
suffer, that by his death he might set
free them who believed on thee. Who,

when he was betrayed to his willing
death, that he might bring to nought
death, and break the bonds of the devil,
and tread hell under foot, and give light
to the righteous, and set up a boundary
post, and manifest his resurrection,
taking bread and giving thanks to thee
said: Take, eat: this is my body, which is
broken for you. As often as ye perform
this, perform my memorial.

Having in memory, therefore, his death
and resurrection, we offer to thee the
bread and the cup, yielding thee thanks,
because thou hast counted us worthy to
stand before thee and to minister to
thee.

And we pray thee that thou wouldest
send thy Holy Spirit upon the offerings
of thy holy church; that thou, gathering
them into one, would grant to all thy
saints who partake to be filled with the
Holy Spirit, that their faith may be
confirmed in truth, that we may praise
and glorify thee. Through thy Servant
Jesus Christ, through whom be to thee
glory and honour, with the Holy Spirit

in the holy church, both now and always and world without end. Amen.[24]

The list could go on. For *sixteen hundred years* the Church of God worshiped liturgically, following the same shape, the same structure, the same flow of drama, as the early Church. Even after the Reformation of the 16th Century, *most* Christians continued to worship God in this way. Roman Catholics, Orthodox, Anglicans, Lutherans - the list can go on - *still* worship God in this way!

Heavenly Worship

Why? Why has *all* the Church for the first sixteen hundred years and *most* of the Church since then worshiped God according to some ancient pattern? I would suggest it is not because the Church is stuffy and stuck in the past, but because the worship of the Church is a copy of heavenly worship, and the worship around the Throne of God is liturgical, and centered on the sacrifice of the Lamb of God. Every glimpse of heavenly worship that we find in the Bible is ordered and liturgical.

---

[24] *The Apostolic Tradition of Hippolytus*, translated by Burton Scott Easton; Cambridge; Archon Press by special arrangement with Cambridge University Press; 1962; p. 35f.

When Isaiah is lifted into the heavenly
realm and sees the worship around God's
throne, he is overwhelmed by the worship of
the angels:

> In the year that King Uzziah died, I
> saw the Lord seated on a throne, high
> and exalted, and the train of his robe
> filled the temple. Above him were
> seraphs, each with six wings: With
> two wings they covered their faces,
> with two they covered their feet, and
> with two they were flying. And they
> were calling to one another: "Holy,
> holy, holy is the LORD Almighty; the
> whole earth is full of his glory" (Isaiah
> 6.1-3).

Read on and you see the scene complete with
incense and an altar. When John was taken up
into heaven, in the book of the Revelation, he
too saw angels and saints singing antiphonal
songs of praise, bowing, burning incense, and
all focusing on the Lamb who was slain:

> After this I looked, and there before
> me was a door standing open in
> heaven. And the voice I had first heard
> speaking to me like a trumpet said,
> "Come up here, and I will show you

what must take place after this." At once I was in the Spirit, and there before me was a throne in heaven with someone sitting on it. And the one who sat there had the appearance of jasper and carnelian. A rainbow, resembling an emerald, encircled the throne. Surrounding the throne were twenty-four other thrones, and seated on them were twenty-four elders. They were dressed in white and had crowns of gold on their heads...In the center, around the throne, were four living creatures...Day and night they never stop saying: "Holy, holy, holy is the Lord God Almighty, who was, and is, and is to come." Whenever the living creatures give glory, honor and thanks to him who sits on the throne and who lives for ever and ever, the twenty-four elders fall down before him who sits on the throne, and worship him who lives for ever and ever. They lay their crowns before the throne and say: "You are worthy, our Lord and God, to receive glory and honor and power, for you created all things, and by your will they were created and have their being" (Revelation 4.1-11).

Then I saw a Lamb, looking as if it had been slain, standing in the center of the throne, encircled by the four living creatures and the elders. He had seven horns and seven eyes, which are the seven spirits of God sent out into all the earth. He came and took the scroll from the right hand of him who sat on the throne. And when he had taken it, the four living creatures and the twenty-four elders fell down before the Lamb. Each one had a harp and they were holding golden bowls full of incense, which are the prayers of the saints. And they sang a new song: "You are worthy to take the scroll and to open its seals, because you were slain, and with your blood you purchased men for God from every tribe and language and people and nation. You have made them to be a kingdom and priests to serve our God, and they will reign on the earth." Then I looked and heard the voice of many angels, numbering thousands upon thousands, and ten thousand times ten thousand. They encircled the throne and the living creatures and the elders. In a loud voice they sang: "Worthy is the Lamb, who was slain, to receive power and wealth and wisdom and strength and honor and glory and praise!" Then I heard every creature in heaven and on earth and under the earth and on the sea, and all that is in them, singing: "To him who sits on the throne and to the Lamb be praise and honor and glory and power, for ever and ever!" The four living creatures said, "Amen," and the elders fell down and worshiped (Revelation 5.1-13).[25]

The book of Hebrews tells us that earthly worship is a copy of heavenly worship (8.5, 9.24). It says that that the angels are God's liturgists - "In speaking of the angels he says, 'He makes his angels winds, his ministers [*leitourgos;* in the Old Testament the word is used only of the Levites and priesthood] flames of fire'" (1.7). But here is the *stunning* part: the book of Hebrews also tells us that the resurrected and ascended *Jesus Christ is doing liturgy in heaven*! "But the ministry [*leitourgia*] Jesus has received is as superior to theirs as the covenant of which he is mediator is superior to the old one..." (8.6). When we worship God on earth, we are joining with Jesus Christ and all the heavenly hosts in a

---

[25] For a study of the Book of Revelation as a liturgical worship service, see Hahn, Scott, *The Lamb's Supper*, New York; Doubleday; 1999.

never-ending liturgy of praise and thanksgiving; "day and night they never stop saying, 'Holy, holy, holy is the Lord God Almighty, who was, and is, and is to come" (Revelation 4.8).

It isn't up to the whims of a leader or the fancy of a culture to determine what constitutes worship. We are to copy what goes on in heaven; we are to join in with the heavenly worship. "But I don't *like* liturgy," some might say, "it doesn't do anything for me." The truth is, you don't have to like liturgy (and for that matter, some things are worth learning to like!). Worship is not *for* people, it is for God. It isn't people-centered, not even godly-people-centered. It is centered on the Lamb. Worship isn't supposed to be what *we* like, it is supposed to be what God calls for. It is for an audience of One. We join with "angels and archangels and all the company of heaven" when we come to the Lord's Table, the Altar of Mercy, and proclaim, "Holy, holy, holy is the Lord God Almighty!"

Chapter Nine

A Four Act Play:
The Shape Of The Liturgy

The Scene: Four friends - two young women, a
young man, and an older man - sitting in
the evening on the patio of an avant
garde coffee shop, sipping espressos and
lattes, the old man smoking a cigar.

The Cast:

Nathan: a 28 year old bohemian looking college
student, who is also a deacon in the
Church.
Megan: a mid-twenties happily married mother
of two.
Ryan: a twenty year old student and waitress,
in love with a rock band guitarist and
singer.
Ken: an early fifties clergyman who is a friend
of the three.

* * * * *

Ryan (holding a CD in her hands): I can't
            believe you waited until this album came
            out on CD. You could have downloaded it
            from the internet a month ago!

Nathan: Word! I haven't bought an entire
            album, even from the internet, in over
            three years. I just download the songs I
            like.

Ryan: Don't you know albums are going the way
            of the dinosaur - even CDs are on their
            way out.

Ken: Well, if that's true, it makes me sad,
            because an entire art form is going to be
            lost in the mix. I guess I'm going the way
            of the dinosaur too.

Megan: But Ken, with the internet, you can just
            download the MP3s that you LIKE. You
            don't have to spend your money on the
            songs you don't like. With a CD you have
            to buy the whole package, like it or not.

Ken: I know, Meg, but haven't you ever bought
            an album, and maybe one of the songs
            you didn't care for at all - at first - ended
            up becoming your favorite cut from the
            whole album?

Megan, Nathan, Ryan: NO!

Ryan: And what are you talking about, "an art form will be lost?" The songs will still be there if you want them, you just don't HAVE to get them.

Ken: The art form I'm talking about is the concept album. I bet none of you have ever even HEARD a concept album.

Megan: You, old man, are treating us like we're children! You're so condescending, (in mocking voice): "I bet none of you have ever even HEARD of a concept album."

Ryan: Uhhh....what's a concept album?

Nathan: Come on, Ryan - everybody knows what a concept album is...

Ken: See, here's my point played out in real life - Ryan doesn't know what it is, because the thing is headed toward extinction. Pretty soon concept albums will be relics; the next generation will never even see a real one!

Megan: You guys back off! Ryan, a concept album is a record or a CD where all the songs tie together. They connect. They tell a story. The whole album is one piece of work, like a movie or a play.

Ken: Exactly, Megan! That's what I love about them; they tell a great story. I can pop one into my car CD player and listen for

an hour as the story unfolds - it's better
than books on CD!

Ryan: Oh! I know what you're talking about! So,
Dark Side Of The Moon, that's a concept
album, right?

Ken and Nathan nod, Megan looks puzzled.

Nathan: Pink Floyd! Word!

Ken: Yes, exactly, Ryan; that's probably the
greatest concept album in rock history.

Ryan: So it's a 70's rock and roll thing? Well, no
wonder its going the way of the
dinosaur! That music is so passe. Only
you old fogies get into it - Boston, The
Eagles, The Rolling Stones - they're all
ANCIENT! Hey, have you guys heard of
the band A Bullet For Pretty Boy? Now
THAT is some great music!

Megan: Oh, Ryan, it's just because you're dating
the lead singer!

Ken: No, Ryan, it's not just a rock and roll thing,
concept albums can be found in every
genre. One of the best ever done was by
Willie Nelson and it was pure country
music: The Red Headed Stranger.

Nathan: Never heard of it. What's it about?

Ken: Man, it's this great story of a preacher
back in the Old West days. His wife leaves

him for another man, so he quits preaching and goes to killing - his wife, the other man, and a bunch of other people. He shot one woman just for touching his horse! There's just a blackness in his heart. Then he meets a good woman and is kind of redeemed by her love. Good story. It could be - well, actually it was - made into a movie.

Ryan: The only thing I know by Willie Nelson is Blue Eyes Crying In The Rain.

Ken: My point exactly! That song is from Red Headed Stranger. Everyone knows that song, but no one knows its setting - its context. No one knows it's about the preacher having to say goodbye for a while to the woman who redeemed him.

Nathan: Well, I hate to be a snob, but I'm not much into 80's rock OR country music. I prefer classical myself.

Megan: Well, Nathan, you may hate to be a snob but you ARE a snob!

Ken: Nathan, my man, I'm convinced that concept albums ORIGINATED in classical music! Handel's Messiah is one of the best. I mean, people who only know the Hallelujah Chorus just think they know Handel - but Messiah is a three hour worship event! It tells the whole story from the birth to the resurrection of

Jesus; it's the whole Gospel done in...well...in a concept album!

Nathan: Ah, I see what you mean - well, in that case all the great classical liturgical stuff - Mozart's Requiem Mass in D Minor, Bach's Mass in B Minor, Rachmaninoff's Vespers - they're ALL concept albums!

Ken: Bingo! Because the act of worship ITSELF is a concept album! I mean, unfortunately, some churches do only one piece or another, kind of like downloading their favorite parts, but worship is supposed to be a whole drama - maybe a musical - with acts and scenes, all played out to the glory of God!

Megan: Dude, you should write a book about it!

Nathan: Word!

* * * * *

Christian worship - and by that I mean the *form* of Christian worship which has its roots in the Old Testament and in the Apostles and has been handed down from them to us through an unbroken line of faithful believers - isn't just a few songs and prayers followed by a sermon. And it certainly isn't a non-participatory event where people go to be entertained or educated. Too many Christians have heard only a piece or two of Christian worship and have not experienced the entire drama. And Christian worship *is* a drama.

Before looking at the actual structure of Christian worship - and I know it has been a long time coming - we need to see one more important development in how the Old Covenant believers worshiped, and consequently how Jesus and the Apostles worshiped. There were actually two parts, two strands, in Jewish worship, one localized to Jerusalem, and one scattered wherever the Jews went.

The Temple And The Synagogue

After the Children of Israel had come into the Promised Land, the time eventually came for them to take down and put away the Tabernacle, and to build God a Temple of stone. The Tabernacle had served as a kind of "motor home" for God! As the people of Israel traveled through the desert and made their way into Canaan, the Tabernacle, a tent of divine design, was pitched and broken down every time the camp moved. But under Solomon, the Tabernacle was replaced with a Temple. Although it kept the same structure as the Tabernacle, it was no longer made of cloth and animal skins; it was a permanent dwelling for the Glory of God, in a house of wood and stone. It was here in the Temple that sacrifices were offered. The Jews didn't make sacrifices in their villages or cities; they traveled to Jerusalem and offered their sacrifices at the hands of the Levites. This is important: *Temple worship was sacrificial worship.*

But there was a local place of worship too. The people gathered, every Sabbath, in *synagogues* (actually a Greek word, not Hebrew, which means *gathering together*). What happened in the synagogue was not unlike what happens in many Protestant churches today: songs were sung, prayers were prayed, Scriptures were read, and sermons were preached.

At first, until they were driven out, the early Christians continued in these two places of worship. If they were in Jerusalem, they would go to the Temple to pray; if they were elsewhere, they would make it their habit to go to synagogue. In fact, Saint Paul's mode of operation was to find the synagogue in whatever city he visited, and because he was a rabbi, he would be given the courtesy of preaching. Of course, what he had to say more often than not got him stoned or thrown out of the city, but this is how the early Church was birthed. Almost immediately, the Christians experienced the severing of their umbilical cord to Judaism. And what took the place of the synagogue was the Christian assembly, often meeting in the homes, and led by priests ordained by the Apostles.

In these newly formed Christian assemblies, the worship of Temple and synagogue were combined; the worship of the first Christians was synagogue-styled: singing, praying, reading, preaching (again, the typical Protestant form) *and* Temple-styled: the offering of the great once-and-for-all sacrifice of Jesus Christ for the sins of the world through the celebration of Holy Communion. Putting it all together created four movements of worship; a four act play of praise and thanksgiving.

The Four Acts Of The Play

A theatrical play can have any number of acts, but most of them are three acts (some are as many as five). The first act is usually introductory, setting the stage for what follows. The second act is usually the most interesting, because it has conflict and dilemma. The third act is resolution, when everything comes together.

The Christian drama of redemption has four acts:

Act One:	Entrance
Act Two:	The Service of the Word (synagogue)
Act Three:	The Service of the Table (Temple)
Act Four:	Dismissal

What follows is a brief description of each act. If you worship in a liturgical church, pay close attention next Sunday morning, and you will find yourself participating in each act of the play. Whether you are in a church that uses the Roman Rite, the 1928 Book of Common Prayer, the 1979 Book of Common Prayer, or some other faithful liturgy, these acts will be obvious.

Act One: Entrance

The first act is about entering into the presence of God. You may notice that the priest and clergy, and perhaps the acolytes, process in wearing white robes. These robes are not the distinguishing garb of clergy, they are baptismal robes - if it were feasible, every member of the congregation would walk in wearing white robes - we are all saints, washed white through the blood of Christ. But since it isn't feasible, a small group which represents everyone else processes in - robed in white.

Act One is the people of God *entering* into the presence of God. It is us coming into the Throne Room of the King. It is the saints of God on earth joining with the saints and angels in glory; joining in with the worship that is always and forever being celebrated by the company of heaven. In this part of the drama we declare what we are here to do - bless God and give thanks to him; we hear it proclaimed that we come into his presence only through his mercy (sometimes the Ten Commandments are read, or else the summary of the Law, and then we pray for God's mercy - *kyrie eleison*). This short act ends with the opening prayer, the collect of the day.

Act Two: The Service Of The Word

Act Two is the longest act of the drama, and it centers on the Word of God. Here is synagogue worship, brought over into the Christian faith. First there are the readings; usually a reading from the Old Testament, the response of a Psalm, a reading of an Epistle, and the reading of the Gospel - the story of Jesus. Usually the Gospel book is taken from the altar, processed down the aisle, and is read from the midst of the congregation; it is, after all, about God being "among us" - Immanuel.

Another part of Act Two is the Creed. Some churches proclaim the Creed before the sermon, and some wait until after the sermon, but the Creed is always proclaimed as a summary of all the Bible has to say. When we say the Creed we are exclaiming to ourselves, to others, to every demon within earshot, and to God, that our faith is rooted in the mighty acts of God through Christ: creation, redemption and the anticipation of our resurrection to eternal life.

The sermon is an important part of the Service of the Word. During this scene the pastor takes a portion of the Scriptures that have been read and expounds on them, applying them to the lives of the people and teaching the deeper insights of the Word of God.

Act Two usually concludes with the Prayers of the People. Rather than just bidding people to pray whatever they want to, this scene continues the tradition of the synagogue and the early Church of praying *the* prayers - a set of prayers covering everything from the evangelization of the world to our nation and our church, to our own personal needs. Ordered prayer helps us to pray for things we might not personally be mindful of. These are not the prayers of a group of individuals who happen to all be in one room at the same time, they are *the* prayers of *the* people of God.

Often included in the Prayers of the People, or else saved for Act Three, is the confession of sins. Having heard the Word of God declared and expounded, the people confess their sins and hear the words of absolution - that in Christ their sins are not only forgiven, but "untied" from them. They are called to walk in the *freedom* of the children of God.

As a kind of interlude (and again, sometimes saved for later in the service), the people, all playing their roles as worshipers and saints of God, are invited to share the Peace of Christ with one another. In this scene we greet one another with the words, "The peace of the Lord be with you," forgiving any offenses against us, that we might come to the Table of the Lord together in unity.

Act Three: The Service Of The Table

We arrive now at the central act of Christian worship, celebrating the death, resurrection, ascension and coming again of Jesus Christ our Lord. There are several scenes in this part of the liturgy, all leading up to the moment when we receive the Sacrament of the Body and Blood of Christ.[26] Here, then are the scenes:

The Sursum Corda   The celebrant (a priest or bishop) invites the people into the Holy of Holies, so to speak. In the Old Covenant only the High Priest could enter into the Holy of Holies, and he only once a year. In the New Covenant, the veil that separated the people from the very dwelling place of God has been removed, and we "approach the throne of grace with confidence, so that we may receive mercy and find grace to help us in our time of need" (Hebrews 4.16). The *Sursum Corda* (Latin for "lift up your hearts") is this:

> Priest: The Lord be with you.
> *People: And with your spirit.*
> Priest: Lift up your hearts.
> *People: We lift them up to the Lord.*
> Priest: Let us give thanks to the Lord
>   our God.

---

[26] This Sacrament will be explored in more detail in Chapter 14.

People: It is right to give him thanks and praise.

The Sanctus   The people of God, having lifted up their hearts to the Lord (having ascended into the heavenly Holy of Holies), now join in with the song that is always being sung around the Throne of God. We join with angels and archangels and all the company of heaven, singing out,

> Holy, holy, holy, Lord God Almighty; Heaven and earth are full of your glory! Hosanna in the highest!

The Canon   The Canon, or the Eucharistic Prayer, is one long prayer that proclaims thanks to God for creating us, declares that we humans have fallen away from God and rejoices in the Father for sending his Son to die and rise again for us and to reconcile us to the Father.

If the entire drama of our redemption is a four act play, the Eucharistic Prayer follows the fourfold pattern of Christ at the Last Supper. He *took, blessed, broke,* and *gave* the bread and the wine. In this prayer, the priest uses the very words of Christ, and mystically stands in his place proclaiming the *Words of Institution*, that Jesus, who on the night he was betrayed took bread; and when he had given you thanks he broke it, and gave it to his disciples, saying, "Take, eat. This is my body which is given for you. Do this in remembrance of me."

After supper, he took the cup, and again giving you thanks he gave it to his disciples, saying, "Drink from this, all of you. This is my blood of the new covenant which is shed for you and for many for the forgiveness of sins. Do this, as often as you drink it, in remembrance of me."

Usually following the *Words of Institution*, the priest invokes the Holy Spirit to "come down upon" (*epiclesis* in Greek) the bread and the wine, making them to be the Body and the Blood of our Lord Jesus Christ. The *Words of Institution* and the *Epiclesis* are not magic, but they are sacramental and covenantal. Here we enter into the remembrance (*anamnesis*)[27] of Christ's sacrifice for us.

This full and wonderful Eucharistic Prayer is concluded with *the Amen*. Saint Paul

---

[27] cf. page 241f.

speaks of believers adding "the Amen" to the prayer of thanksgiving offered by the priest (1 Corinthians 14.16, 2 Corinthians 1.20). The whole Eucharistic Prayer is concluded by a great "Amen!" when the people of God make the entire prayer their own by adding this covenant-making word.

The Lord's Prayer   After the Eucharistic Prayer, the Our Father is prayed by all the faithful, again praying as our Lord taught us to pray, and using his own words in the presence of the Father.

The Fraction   Remember the fourfold pattern Jesus used at the Last Supper (and on the Road to Emmaus; cf. Luke 24.30)? Jesus *took* (the priest takes the bread in the Eucharistic prayer), *blessed* (the priest blesses the bread and wine in the *Word of Institution* and the *Epiclesis*), then Jesus *broke* the bread. At the *Fraction*, the priest follows the pattern of Jesus and breaks the bread, just as Christ's body was broken for us, which leads to the fourth action of Jesus. He *gave* the bread of his Body to the disciples.

The Communion   During a sad era of the Church, in Medieval times, most Christians didn't actually receive communion. They counted themselves unworthy (having not been taught the grace and mercy of God), and so they often *went* to Communion but seldom *received* Communion. In this part of the service we receive the Body and Blood of Jesus Christ into ourselves, body, soul and spirit. This is communion (Greek, *koinonia*[28]) - a participation, a sharing in - the Body and Blood of Christ. Here the great exchange occurs; our weakness for his strength, our brokenness for his wholeness, our sinfulness for his righteousness, our infirmities for his wholeness. Here is the culmination, the pinnacle, the climax of our act of worship. It is *the most intimate moment* of the drama, and the most powerful moment of our worship.

The Post-Communion Prayer After the people have been fed at the Altar of God's mercy, a final prayer is prayed, thanking God once again for feeding us with the Body and Blood of Christ, and asking that he empower us to live for him and serve him. Thus ends Act Three.

Act Four: The Dismissal

The grand climax of the drama is accomplished in Act Three, but the play isn't over yet! The final act is the people being

---

[28] cf. Chapter 13.

blessed, and sent out into the world to take Jesus to others. This short act has three brief scenes.

The Blessing   After communion, the priest or bishop stands before the people, extends his hands over them, and in an action that goes all the way back to the High Priest Aaron, blesses them in the name of the Father and of the Son and of the Holy Spirit. He makes the sign of the cross over them and they "catch it" (like a lover catching a kiss blown from across the room) by crossing themselves.

The Retiring Procession   After the blessing, and usually to a hymn, anthem or song, the priest and others vested to represent the people of God, end the service the way they began it - in procession. Only this time, they are processing out *from* the Altar *into* the world. It is a picture of us expanding the Garden into the howling wilderness, of us expanding the Kingdom of God into the nations. We go out, in the power of the Holy Spirit, to continue our service of God among the people of the earth.

The Dismissal   In the final scene of the drama, a kind of encore, if you will, the deacon (if there is one, otherwise the priest) walks back in to the midst of the congregation and proclaims "Let us bless the Lord!" And the congregation, for one final time, respond with words which capture what the entire service has been about from start to finish: "Thanks be to God! Alleluia! Alleluia!"

Do you see that liturgical worship is not just "a style" of worship that suits some and not others? It is a full-orbed presentation of thanksgiving to the King of Kings and the Lord of Lords. And when he applauds (as the audience of One), the wind that passes between his clapping hands is the wind of the Holy Spirit, rushing out over his people and empowering them for life.

Chapter Ten

Showtunes:
Music in Worship

J.R.R. Tolkien wrote what has been acclaimed in a number of popular surveys as the most important work of fiction in the 20th century, *The Lord of The Rings*. The trilogy, which tells a story filled with wizards and hobbits, ents and dwarves, men and elves, all on a quest to destroy an ancient evil in Middle Earth, has been brought into the realm of theater by the wonderful movies directed by Peter Jackson.

Die-hard Tolkien fans know of another of his works which is a prequel to the trilogy, and though published after Tolkien's death actually predates his more famous work. Tolkien, a devout Christian (and dear friend of

C.S. Lewis) begins *The Silmarillion* with a retelling of the creation story; only, in Tolkien's fiction, God and the angels *sing* the world into creation. Here, then, are the first three paragraphs of *The Silmarillion*.

There was Eru [God], the One, who in Arda [Earth] is called Iluvatar; and he made first the Ainur [angels], the Holy Ones, that were the offspring of his thought, and they were with him before aught else was made. And he spoke to them, propounding to them themes of music; and they sang before him, and he was glad...

...And it came to pass that Iluvatar called together all the Ainur and declared to them a mighty theme, unfolding to them things greater and more wonderful than he had yet revealed; and the glory of its beginning and the splendour of its end amazed the Ainur, so that they bowed before Iluvatar and were silent.

Then Iluvatar said to them, "Of the theme that I have declared to you, I will now that ye make in harmony together a Great Music. And since I have kindled you with the Flame

Imperishable, ye shall show forth your
powers in adorning this theme, each
with his own thoughts and devices, if he
will. But I will sit and hearken, and be
glad that through you great beauty has
been wakened into song."[29]

A page later, God calls the angels
together and shows them what they had sung:

But when they were come
into the Void, Iluvatar said to them:
"Behold your Music!" And he showed
to them a vision, giving to them sight
where before was only hearing; and
they saw a new World made visible
before them, and it was globed amid the
Void, and it was sustained therein, but
was not of it. And as they looked and
wondered this World began to unfold
its history, and it seemed to them that it
lived and grew.[30]

What a beautiful depiction of the story
of Creation. But it doesn't take Tolkien to
convince us that *God loves music*. In *our* book,
the Bible, music plays a role from Genesis

---

[29] Tolkien, J.R.R., *The Silmarillion*, Boston, Houghton
Mifflin Company, 1977, p. 15f.

[30] *ibid*, p. 17.

(4.21) to Revelation (15.3). Music is there in the beginning of our story, and music is there at the end. The Bible even contains, right in the middle (just try opening your Bible to the middle) a songbook - the book of Psalms - containing 150 songs written over a period of 1000 years by at least seven different songwriters. Everywhere you look in the Bible and the history of the Church, God's people have worshiped him through music. It may be African drums or English pipe organs, it may be stately hymns or foot-stomping choruses, but like the music of Tolkien's angels, every song sung by God's people joins with the music of heaven to make an eternal symphony of praise.

Music Is Powerful Stuff

Without the music, the movie *Jaws* would lose about 80% of its fear factor. The music elicits the emotion. Music is so important that in some way it actually becomes a character in the movie; the movie wouldn't be the same or be complete without it. As an exercise, I'm going to list a few movies and invite you to listen in your mind to the soundtrack. Suddenly you will see how important the tune is to the tale: *Star Wars, Out of Africa, Somewhere in Time, Casablanca, The Wizard of Oz, Chariots of Fire*. These movies are made complete by the musical scores which accompany them; the music communicates the emotion of the story directly to the heart in a way that nothing else can, not even great acting, directing or writing.

Of course, the movie theater is not the only place where music is powerful. Another theater - theater of war - has a long history of music, and on the battlefield, music was used not only to communicate but to inspire. When the armies of Israel went forth into battle, the tribe of Judah (which means "praise"), went forth first. My wife's fourth great grandfather was a twelve year old drummer boy in the Revolutionary War, taking music into the field of battle. In World War One the British troops were led into battle by the kilt-clad bagpipers of the Scottish Highland Regiments, called by the Germans, 'The Ladies from Hell", soldiers so tough they could cross-dress and still be fierce warriors!

Special dinners are made all the more romantic by the ensemble in the corner playing *Besame Mucho*; the President of the United States is greeted by the striking up of the band playing *Hail To The Chief*; the parties we have to mark the passing of our years would be incomplete without a rousing round of *Happy Birthday To You*. Music permeates our lives - it fills our entertainment, our war, our grief, our love. Music affects people.

It also fills our worship. One of the reasons music is so important in worship is because it is so memorable. The early heresies knew this, and set their doctrine to music (so, by the way, do the modern heresies. As a young man I was visited by Mormon missionaries who told me of God's wife - Mother God, I suppose; when I pressed them for a biblical source for this belief, or even a *Book of Mormon* reference, they were reluctant to admit that the only source they had for the doctrine was their hymnbook!).

When Saint Paul encouraged the Christians in Ephesus to, *"Speak to one another* with psalms, hymns and spiritual *songs"* (Ephesians 5.19), he recognized the horizontal, believer-to-believer impact of singing. Songs encourage, edify and teach truth to the actors in the drama of worship.

When Martin Luther penned the words to *A Mighty Fortress Is Our God*, he made them easily remembered by setting them to music with a borrowed (and slowed down) tavern tune that everyone already knew. John and Charles Wesley wrote over 6000 hymns to help not only faithful churchgoers but also coalminers and street sweepers who attended their open air meetings to remember their message of grace.[31] As one Southern Baptist so aptly said, "I have heard thousands of sermons in my life and cannot remember a single line from any of them, but start me out and I'll sing at least one verse from every song in the *Broadman Hymnal!*"

What Manner of Music?

Some Christians tend to view a particular style of music as holy or sacred, and relegate other styles as either worldly, irrelevant or outmoded. This sword of judgmental attitude cuts both ways - those who prefer reverent hymns look down their noses at drums and guitars in the church, while those who embrace contemporary music shake their heads at the irrelevance of ancient hymnody.

David Osterlund, a missionary to Ethiopia, recounts asking a Coptic priest for permission to perform Handel's *Messiah* in his church, "with an Ethiopian orchestra of strings, brass and percussion musicians he had

---

[31] Incidentally, it is ironic that Methodist hymnals have chosen to leave out many of the Wesleys' eucharistic hymns on the grounds that they are "too Catholic."

gathered together and trained. The priest replied that percussion and brass would be acceptable, 'but strings', he said, 'absolutely not! Don't you know strings belong in the beer halls, not the church?'"[32] What is accepted as traditional in Europe is considered scandalous in Africa!

I would suggest that judgmental camps on all sides are wrong, and that they miss an important principle: God has redeemed and sanctified all human giftedness, and all cultures (not just Latin American or African or Western European or Asian, but also the subcultures of a given society) can channel their creativity to the glory of God.

I recall, as a teenager in the days of the "Jesus Movement" of the 1970s, when young people from the "hippie generation" were coming to Christ and bringing their rock music with them, that books were written and sermons were preached decrying the style of music these kids were using to praise God. The issue wasn't the lyrics, but the style - the *beat*. I actually read a book which sought to prove that the very beat of pop music was "of the devil" because it stirred the *soul* (not, mind

[32] Liesch, Barry, *People In The Presence Of God*, Grand Rapids, MI, 1988, p. 195.

you, the *spirit*) and this was a soulish, evil thing! Well, some souls need stirring, and God is the one who created our emotions, and created them to be touched by music. It reminds me of the story Barry Liech tells of his brother and himself learning how to play the Jamaican rumba, and coming up with a clarinet-piano arrangement for the gospel song *There's a New Song in my Heart.* "After the service an elderly woman expressed her appreciation to us: 'Boys, that song of yours was just *wonderful*! It was so lively! I could feel the joy of the Lord in you...' I am glad she felt this way, because there was joy in us....Silently though, I said to myself, 'Ma'am, a lot of that "joy of the Lord" you are experiencing is the rumba.'"[33]

So, a church may choose to use only traditional hymns and that is good and fine, or a church may choose to use contemporary music and that is good and fine, but a church should not think itself more righteous or God pleasing than its neighbor churches because of the *style* of music with which it worships. When C.S. Lewis expounded on the music wars in the Church of his day, he wrote, "The first and most solid conclusion which (for me) emerges is that both musical parties, the High

---

[33] *ibid*, p. 198.

Brows and the Low, assume far too easily the spiritual value of the music they want."[34]

Lewis had something of an epiphany in this regard when he wrote, in a rather cranky mood, "I naturally *loathe* nearly all hymns; the face and life of the charwoman in the next pew who revels in them, teach me that good taste in poetry or music are not necessary to salvation."[35] And *this* was about classic Anglican hymnody!

When our congregation, Christ Church in Sherman, Texas, was first born, we invited the renown worship writer Robert Webber to visit our church and teach our people. He so graciously accepted the invitation and came for a weekend of inspiring instruction. One of the things Dr. Webber taught us was, if we were going to have contemporary music that we should put it "up front" and do it before the liturgy actually began. That is not at all how we had been doing it, and we almost changed the service that Sunday in order to fit his recommendations. Then we thought, how can he give us an honest critique if we don't do

[34] Lewis, C.S., *On Church Music*, in *Christian Reflections*, Grand Rapids, MI, Eerdmans, 1994 (orig. 1949), p. 96.

[35] Lewis, C.S., *Letters of C.S. Lewis*, New York, Mariner Books, 1975, p. 224.

what we always do? So we kept to our pattern, the praise music placed right in the middle of the service with additional pieces scattered here and there throughout the service, and cautiously awaited Webber's critique. On the way back to the airport I asked him for an honest assessment. "I wouldn't change a thing," he said, "In fact, you have given me a new model to work from!" My jaw nearly dropped, but Webber saw that it *worked*. And it *does* work. It is not a question of style - it works with Latin, country, pop, classical, African, Chinese, Island music (you get the point) - it is a matter of intention and heartfelt devotion. The adoration of God throughout Scripture, whether it be Old Testament worship around the Ark of the Covenant, New Testament worship around the Table of the Lord, Paul and Silas singing hymns of praise in a midnight jail cell, or heaven itself filled with the songs of saints and angels, is always worship permeated with music.

Psalms, Hymns And Spiritual Songs

When Paul wrote to the Church in Ephesus, he told them to, "Speak to one another in *psalms, hymns and spiritual songs*. Sing and make music in your hearts to the Lord, always

173

giving thanks to God the Father for everything, in the name of our Lord Jesus Christ." (Ephesians 5.19f). We have already noted the horizontal aspect of music ("speak to one another), but there is also a vertical aspect: "to the Lord." Keeping in mind that our entire act of worship is for an Audience of One, our music must not be seen as entertainment for the congregation. Instead, the choir, the soloist, the singing group, the orchestra, the band, the organist, the pianist, and the whole congregation are all performing for the King; the songs are directed to the Throne.

Paul specifically mentions three kinds of songs, and while he was not giving a lesson in hymnody, it is worth emphasizing his distinctions.

Psalms obviously bring to mind the book of Psalms, and indeed this book was the first songbook of the Church. These songs speak to every occasion of life including the best and the worst of times. They often express our hearts condition better than our own words can, and uniquely in regard to songs, they are not only man's words, but God's Word! The early Church understood the book of Psalms as Christ centered (for example, when Psalm 1 declares

"Blessed is *the man*...," the early Church understood "the man" to be Jesus). And most importantly, even if the Psalms dealt with the ups and downs of life, they were ultimately God directed songs of praise and thanksgiving, extolling his greatness in power and mercy.

This is not to say that *all* our *psalms* are taken from the ancient Hebrew book, but it does serve as a foundation and model for the songs which emerge from our own times.

Hymns bring to mind the traditional music of the Church. But hymns include more than the well loved songs of the Wesleys and Isaac Watts. The oldest hymn outside the New Testament, already called ancient by St. Basil the Great (who died in 379), is the *Phos Hilaron*, or *Oh Gracious Light*. Following on in the march of Christian history we discover the emergence of chant, the great hymns of Medieval times (for example, the 7th Century *All Glory, Laud and Honor*), the music of the Reformation and the English revivals of Wesley and Whitefield, the evangelical and gospel songs of the 19th and early 20th Centuries (Fanny Crosby's *Blessed Assurance, I Am Thine O Lord,* and *Redeemed How I Love To Proclaim It* come to mind, to mention but a few of her

9000 hymns) and the modern era which has already produced timeless classics such as Andrea Crouch's *To God Be The Glory* and Michael W. Smith's *Worthy Is The Lamb*.

The point being, the Church is alive and so is its music. Godly creativity didn't die with Charles Wesley or Fannie Crosby, and it won't die with the Newsboys or Juan Luis Guerra![36] Congregations should use music from the whole spectrum of Church history - it is all *our* music. We ought to sing the *Phos Hilaron*, the majestic hymns of centuries past, the gospel songs of the evangelical world, and the praise choruses of today. The "old stuff" might be likened to good wine and cheese which gets better with age; the "new stuff," some of which will be shortlived, can be likened to fresh fruit; but together they serve up a wonderful feast of praise.

Spiritual Songs, the third kind of singing mentioned by Saint Paul is also the most enigmatic and controversial. Some have said that these spiritual songs were simply songs sung with a spiritual intention - but wouldn't all the psalms and hymns be sung with that same intention? At the risk of being

---

[36] If you haven't heard his *Gloria*, you should. Find the cover version by The Brooklyn Tabernacle Choir.

labeled a raving Charismatic, I'm going to go out on a limb, but I'll be sitting on that limb with the likes of Jerome and Augustine. I suggest to you that spiritual songs are songs given by the Holy Spirit *in the moment*. These songs may be in a known human language, or in an unknown heavenly language.

In the Psalms, David mentions repeatedly the *new song*. "I will sing a *new song* to you, O God; on the ten-stringed lyre I will make music to you..." (Psalm 144.9).[37] During the time of David, when the choirs stood before the Ark of the Covenant in the Tabernacle of David and sang in shifts all day and all night, recorders were appointed to write down the new songs which were birthed, spontaneously, as people worshiped in the Presence of God.

In the book of Revelation John saw a vision of heavenly worship where the priests around the throne, "sang *a new song*: 'You are worthy to take the scroll and to open its seals...'" (Revelation 5.9). Here is a song which hadn't been sung before - not until this moment in John's vision, and in response to what God was doing at that very time. So, a spiritual song may well be a new song, given

---

[37] cf. Psalm 33.3, 40.3, 96.1, 98.1, 149.1

by the Holy Spirit for the edification of the people and the praise of God.

But there is also a kind of spiritual singing which Saint Paul mentions in his first letter to the Church in Corinth: "For if I pray in a tongue, my spirit prays, but my mind is unfruitful. So what shall I do? I will pray with my spirit, but I will also pray with my mind; I will *sing with my spirit*, but I will also sing with my mind" (1 Corinthians 14.14f).

Add one more crazy Charismatic item: shouting. I know that no proper Anglican church would ever shout during a service, but listen to what the Word of God says:

Shout for joy to the Lord, all the earth (Psalm 100.1).

Shout with joy to God, all the earth! Sing the glory of his name; make his praise glorious! (Psalm 66.1f).

Sing to him a *new song*; play skillfully, and *shout* for joy (Psalm 33.3).

O come, let us sing for joy to the Lord, Let us *shout* joyfully to the rock of our salvation. Let us come before his presence with thanksgiving, Let us *shout* joyfully to him with psalms (Psalm 95.1f).

When Jerome translated the Bible into Latin, he translated "shout joyfully" as *jubilatio*, "loud shouting or whooping." Jerome wrote, "By the term *jubilus* we understand that which neither in words nor syllables nor letters nor speech is possible to express or comprehend how much man ought to praise God."[38]

Jerome isn't alone in this. No less a stellar figure than Saint Augustine himself tells us of this phenomenon:

I am about to say what ye already know. One who jubilates, uttereth not words, but it is a certain sound of joy without words...A man rejoicing in his own exultation, after certain words which cannot be uttered or understood, bursteth forth into sounds of exultation without words, so that it seemeth that he indeed doth rejoice with his voice itself, but as if filled with excessive joy cannot express

---

[38] *Patrologia Latina*, v. 26, p. 970; quoted in Webber, Robert, *The Complete Library of Christian Worship*, Nashville, Star Song, 1994, v. 4, p. 282.

in words the subject of that joy...When then are we jubilant? When we praise that which cannot be uttered.[39]

In all these things shall we not rejoice? Or shall we contain our joy? Or shall words suffice for our gladness? Or shall the tongue be able to express our rejoicing? If therefore no words suffice, "Blessed is the people, O Lord, who knoweth glad shouting [*jubilatio*]."[40]

Space does not permit to quote Cassiodorus, Isadore of Seville, John Chrysostom, Theodoret, John Cassian, Bonaventure and a host of others. Suffice it to say that jubilation permeated the life and writings of the saints of the Church from Saint Paul forward. During the first nine centuries of Church history jubilation was "standard practice." The Pentecostal and Charismatic movements of the 20th Century, while themselves filled with many false starts and erroneous teachings, have to their credit seen the recovery of spiritual songs. It remains to

---

[39] Augustine, *Expositions on the Book of Psalms*, Shaff, Philip, editor, *The Nicene and Post-Nicene Fathers, First Series*, Grand Rapids, MI, Eerdmans, 1983 (1888), Volume 8, p. 488.

[40] *ibid*, p. 433.

future generations to restore jubilation to its proper place in the context of liturgy. If you are uncomfortable with this, it's OK; some people are also uncomfortable with incense and candles and written prayers. But, to reprise Augustine, quoting David (Psalm 89.15), "Blessed is the people, O Lord, who know how to jubilate."

St. Gregory the Great said that jubilation is the praise of the blessed in heaven. I had a Baptist minister once tell me that he never understood the verse in Revelation where John wrote, "His feet were like bronze glowing in a furnace, and his voice was like the sound of rushing waters" (1.16), until he heard for the first time a large crowd of Christians singing in the Spirit. It was, he said, the sound of heaven. And yet, when we come together as the Church, isn't that exactly where we are? Don't we enter God's Throne Room? Aren't we surrounded by angels and archangels and all the company of heaven? And there - *here* - we are invited to add our voices to the never ending *new song* that only the redeemed can sing.

Singing With Great Gusto

Finally, a word about *how* we sing songs - whether they be hymns, chants, gospel songs or choruses. There is nothing more disheartening than standing in a congregation full of people who *mumble* their praises to God! Bad actors are what they are. If they were on Broadway they would be fired in no time!

Augustine complained about the apathy of singing in his own churches and said that such lackluster singing gave an open door for the more exciting cultists of the day:

> In Africa the members of the Church are rather too indifferent in regard to it; on which account the Donatists reproach us with our grave chanting of the divine songs of the prophets in our churches, while they inflame their passions in their revels by the singing of psalms of human composition which rouse them like the stirring notes of the trumpet on the battle-field. But when brethren are assembled in the church, why should not the time be devoted to singing of sacred songs, excepting of course while reading or preaching is going on, or while the presiding minister prays aloud, or the united prayer of the congregation is led by the deacon's voice? At the other intervals not thus

occupied, I do not see what could be a more excellent, useful, and holy exercise for a Christian congregation."[41]

John Wesley gave perfect instructions on singing when he directed,

Learn the tunes. Sing them as printed. Sing lustily and with good courage. Beware of singing as if you are half-dead, or half-asleep, but lift your voice with strength. Be no more afraid of your voice, nor more ashamed of its being heard, than when you sing the songs of Satan. Sing modestly. Do not bawl. Make one clear melodious sound. Sing in tune. Above all, sing spiritually. Attend strictly to the sense of what you sing, and see that your heart is not carried away with the sound, but offered to God continually."[42]

My wife Shirley once remarked that she was "singing with great gusto," to which a sarcastic Anglican priest replied, "*You* sang

---

[41] Augustine, Epistle 55.18, Shaff, Philip, editor, *The Nicene and Post Nicene Fathers, First Series*, Grand Rapids, MI, Eerdmans, 1983 (1886), Volume 1, p. 315.

[42] Quoted in Flynn, Leslie B, *Together We Worship*, Wheaton, IL, Victor Books, 1983, p. 87.

with The Great Gusto?" We all laughed at his joke, but perhaps all Christians should take that stage name: The Great Gusto. For we are all called to make his praises glorious, and this can only happen when we sing his praises not only with our lips, but with all our heart.

Chapter Eleven:

Timing Is Everything:
The Church's Year

Time for a quick quiz:

1. What month are you most likely to see scary monster movies on television?
2. When is the best time to catch a live performance of *Scrooge*?
3. When will you see the best fireworks shows, accompanied by razzmatazz patriotic music?

Answers: (1) October, (2) December, (3) July.

Theater, cinema, concerts and television - the performing arts - understand timing, not only in the perfect moment for an actor to deliver his lines, but also in the perfect time to present a show. Scary shows just do better near Halloween; sappy Christmas shows are best, obviously, near Christmas; fireworks and patriotic revues are for the Fourth of July (unless you are from the South, which after the War of Northern Aggression culturally refused to celebrate Independence Day for about 75 years and popped their firecrackers on New Year's Eve instead). But the test is not over yet. One final question - the most important one:

4. Why is it that we have all kinds of special markings of time in the secular world, but not in the Christian world?

Answer: Because the Church has fought against encroaching secularism in practically every area of life, but has surrendered the arena of time to the secular realm, as if this were something left unredeemed by Christ.

I have a pastor friend in my city who often joins with us, a group of local pastors, for weekly prayer. I had to chuckle when I read the announcement that for the upcoming Sunday his text would be "And Mary pondered these things in her heart" (Luke 2.19). What made me laugh is the upcoming Sunday was Mother's Day, and I bet some other clergy friends that (a) this is one of only three "holy days" he celebrated, and (b) other than Christmas it was the only time he preached on the Blessed Virgin Mary! Wait - Mother's Day is a holy day? What am I thinking? Of course it isn't. I am all for Mother's Day, but however wonderful it is, it isn't a holy day to be celebrated in the Church. Now that I have just offended every mother reading this book, please allow me to be an equal opportunity offender: neither should our focus of worship be Father's Day or Grandparent's Day or Boy Scouts' Day or Independence Day or Martin Luther King, Jr. Day. Maybe we should celebrate Cinco De Mayo - well, you catch my drift. Saint Patrick's Day stays, however, because he was a Spirit-filled bishop in the Church of God (*Go Irish!*).

The Church has a calendar, but in many cases it has been relegated to the bin of "stuffy old religion." Many churches celebrate only two days of the entire year, Christmas and Easter, and the vacuum that has been created by the absence of holy occasions has been filled with secular markings of time.

A Biblical View Of Time

Time is, to use an old word, a "creature" of God. God created time; he created the sun and made the Earth revolve around it; he created the seasons; he made the moon with its waxing and waning to mark the months. It reminds me of that great cartoon where God, dusting his hands, tells the angels, "I've just created a twenty-four hour period of time divided into light and dark." When the angels asked what he was going to do now, he replied, "I think I'll call it a day!" "And there was evening and there was morning, the first day" (Genesis 1.5).

If time is a creature of God, then it is part of his redemption as well. It is a "thing," and God's purpose is through Christ "to reconcile to himself all things, whether things on earth or things in heaven, by making peace through his blood, shed on the cross" (Colossians 1.20).

The Greeks saw time as something circular, without beginning and end, and without purpose. There was no goal; time was going nowhere. The Jews, on the other hand, saw time in a linear fashion - time had a destiny, a goal, a fulfillment; and that fulfillment, the Jews believed, would arrive when the Messiah established his Kingdom. Christians believe that Jesus is the Messiah, and that he did establish his Kingdom, and it continues to expand until his return. So Christians live with a kind of already/not-yet tension; Christ has come, but Christ will come again; the Kingdom has come, but not yet. We live between "ages past" and "the age to come;" we live in the final age. We have a point of reference - *in time* - time has been redeemed by our Lord and Savior, and time is going somewhere.

To lay hold of the biblical idea of time, we must distinguish between two kinds of time mentioned in the Scriptures. The first is *chronos*, and this is time as it is measured: Thursday; 2010; 6.24 a.m.; April. "Then Herod called the magi secretly and found from them the exact time (*chronos*) the star had appeared" (Matthew 2.7).

The second kind of time is *kairos*, and this means time, not as it is measured, but as events happen. If I were to ask my family, "Do you remember the time we all packed up and floated on the Frio River?", they would all certainly remember the event, but none of them would respond, "Sure, it was August 12, 2008, at three in the afternoon." They would remember the occasion, not the date. I would be asking them a *kairos* question, not a *chronos* question. I remember (fearfully and dreadfully) one of my father's favorite phrases: "high time." He might say, "It's time to go to bed" and what he would mean was, "It's 10 p.m., the *chronos* for going to bed." But if he discovered, an hour later, that I still hadn't made it to slumberland, he would say, "Kenneth Neal, it's *high time* you get to bed!" What he was saying was, "Kenneth, the *kairos* has arrived for you to get in the bed!"

Chronos, then, is the measuring and marking of *kairos*. *Chronos* is given meaning by *kairos*. One more example. What do these dates mean: June 6, 1944; November 22, 1963; September 11, 2001? Of course, these are just dates - markings - *chronos*. But they are given their meaning by what *happened* - *kairos*: the Normandy Invasion in World War II, the assassination of John F. Kennedy, the destruction of the Twin Towers in New York. When those dates roll around in a sense we re-live the events.

In a secular sense birthdays and anniversaries are *chronos* marking the *kairos* of birth and marriage. In the Church's life we mark the happenings of the life of Jesus, the Apostles, and great men and women of God and in a sense enter into the *moment* - the *kairos* - of those events.

In the Old Testament, time was marked in a weekly fashion with the Sabbath. In creation God gave a pattern of six days of work followed by a day of rest. When he delivered his people from the slavery of Egypt he restored this pattern, to signify that they were no longer slaves (who never had any rest), but covenant people called to a weekly celebration of freedom. There was also an annual cycle of life marked, not by secular or even simply agrarian markings, but by the feasts which celebrated God acting among them: Passover, Pentecost, the Day of Atonement, Hanukkah and other important times of worship and thanksgiving.

In the New Testament we also find a weekly and an annual cycle. The Lord's Day - the first day of the week - marked the event of Jesus rising from the dead and the beginning of the new creation. Annual holy days were also celebrated, the greatest being Easter, or, to use the ancient word, Pascha - the annual celebration of the resurrection of Jesus.

The Benefits Of The Church Year

As the Church developed, and as its worship developed, a pattern of marking time similar to the Old Testament pattern emerged, but the focus was on the important New Covenant events that occurred in the life of Christ and his new people. The celebration of the life of Christ is an instrument that orders our spirituality. As individuals, families and congregations we order our lives in the annual pattern which moves us along from preparing for the birth of Jesus to the culmination of his life and ministry in the resurrection, ascension and sending of the Holy Spirit to empower and guide us.

Several things happen when we intentionally follow the Church year as a congregation and as individuals. First, it gives us a pattern in our devotion, reading and meditation. It provides a rhythm to our spirituality not unlike a great piece of music with its pianissimos, crescendos and rests. The Church year brings us into seasons of intense joy, quiet introspection, and peaceful rest.

Following the Church year also has the effect of involving our lives and not just our minds. The movement of our lives through the year becomes ordered by Christ's life. We read the stories of particular events in the life of Christ, we decorate our homes and churches, we have special meals and celebrations, we even pray different prayers in different seasons, and our faith becomes more than head knowledge. There is a kind of permeation of our whole being that happens when we let our time be shaped by Christ's time.

Another benefit of following the Church year is that we are immersed, year in and year out, with the whole story of Jesus. Having celebrated the Church year for 20 years of my life, after having spent the first 30 in non-liturgical Christian settings, I must confess that I am intimately more aware of the warp and woof of Jesus' life and ministry than I was before. And I am saddened that so many of my Christian friends suffer from a kind of unintentional poverty, a scarcity of hearing, reading and contemplating the mighty acts of God in Christ. Think about it: every year Christians who follow the Church calendar prepare for his coming (the first as a babe, the last as a King), rejoice at his birth, see the Spirit descend at his baptism, listen to him teach, watch him perform miracles, weep at his passion and death and shout aloud at his resurrection and ascension! At the same time, other Christians may go for literally years (or at least until the pastor decides to preach a random sermon) without hearing or thinking about some of these might acts. To demonstrate the point for yourself, ask your Christian friends who worship in nonliturgical churches, when was the last time their pastor's sermon focused on the Ascension, or on the baptism of Jesus.

The final benefit of the Church year is the common focus it provides for individuals, families, congregations and the wider Church. Liturgical Christians around the world celebrate the same seasons and times, giving a common spirituality to folk who may not attend the same church or live in the same city or nation, or belong to the same denomination. I will never forget when, as a young pastor in a non-denominational church, I preached the lectionary without telling anyone. One particular Sunday the Gospel was about when Martha busied herself about the house while Mary sat learning at Jesus feet. It so happened that I decided to preach an "illustrated sermon" that morning, complete with pots and pans and brooms, demonstrating the busy-ness of Martha. The next day, a dear woman in our congregation, whose daughter attended a Methodist church in a nearby town, came to me with a look of utter surprise and said, "Pastor Ken, you'll never believe this - but Susie's pastor preached about *the same thing* you as preached last Sunday, and even had pots and pans to illustrate the sermon!" I just smiled, said nothing, and she chalked the whole thing up to a work of the Holy Spirit. She was right.

The Church calendar is composed of two cycles, with a down-time season of ordinary time between them.

The Christmas Cycle

Advent   The four Sundays before Christmas constitute the season of Advent (which means *coming* or *arrival*), when the focus is on preparing for the coming of the Lord. During this season the readings, prayers and music are full of anticipation and hope, as we give attention to both the first coming of Christ as a baby in Bethlehem, and his Second Coming as King of Kings and Lord of Lords.

Christmas   Have you heard the song, *The Twelve Days of Christmas*? For too many believers Christmas is a single day of family dinners and gift giving, coming on the tail end of an exhausting season of shopping! For liturgical Christians, Christmas is a twelve day season that begins with Christmas Day on December 25.

One of my favorite services of the year is Midnight Mass, when we gather together late at night to celebrate the birth of Jesus. The church is packed full of people singing carols and hearing the Good News of Christ's birth. We share Holy Communion, then we all light and hold candles for a final round of *Joy To The World*. After the service - around one in the morning - it is our family tradition to head from the Church to an all night diner for a very late (or very early) pancake breakfast. I wouldn't miss it for the world.

Gift giving is obviously part of most people's Christmas celebration, but with it being a season instead of a day, gift giving can take on a new dimension. One of the best gives I have ever received came from a woman in our congregation named Toni. At the Midnight Mass service she delivered to me a wicker basket with twelve wrapped gifts to be opened one each day throughout the season. It was a very thoughtfully prepared gift, and I ended up with a travel journal, a travel coffee mug, a book, a CD, and several other small presents. I couldn't wait for each new day to roll around to see what Toni had done this time!

The season of Christmas celebrates the birth of Jesus, the presentation of Christ in the Temple and his being named, and culminates on January 6 with the Feast of the Epiphany, marking the day the wise men arrived to worship the Christ Child, the first Gentiles to serve our Lord Jesus. Epiphany is about the people who walked in darkness seeing a great light, so in our congregation, when weather permits we gather together in a field, sing one last round of Christmas carols, and have a giant bonfire of dry Christmas trees - talk about light in the darkness! Behold, the light of Christ!

Ordinary Time   Between the close of the Christmas Cycle and the beginning of the Easter Cycle (between Epiphany and Ash Wednesday), there are a few weeks of Ordinary Time when the biblical focus is on Christ being manifested to the nations. The Gospels are usually about the miracles and teachings of Christ with no particular events to celebrate - a kind of musical rest after the crescendo of Christmas.

The Easter Cycle

Lent   Beginning with Ash Wednesday, when believers come together to be marked with ashes and reminded of their mortality, the Lenten season covers the forty days before Easter. Lent is just a Latin word for springtime, but for Christians these forty days - correlating to the forty days of Jesus fasting and being tempted in the wilderness - are a time of identifying with Christ by considering our own weaknesses and temptations, and by various fastings and sacrificial acts and gifts.

Holy Week The final week of Lent begins with Palm Sunday, during which we process into the church waving palm branches and proclaiming loud hosannas. On Maundy (Latin for *commandment*) Thursday we gather together to celebrate the night Jesus instituted the Lord's Supper, gave us a new commandment to love one another, and was then betrayed by Judas in the Garden of Gethsemane. After we celebrate the Holy Eucharist, the service ends with the terrible "Stripping of the Altar." While the people stand in silence everything that reminds us of Christ is removed from the church - the cross, the sacred vessels, the altar furnishings. The clergy then remove their stoles and crosses and process out in silence, with nothing but a simple white cloth, the fair linen, remaining on the altar. Midway through this silent procession, I turn, go back to the altar, and violently rip away the fair linen, dragging it on the floor behind me as I depart. I've done this for 20 years and it still sends shivers down my spine. Our people have watched it as many times and are still left standing, as if slapped in the face with the sense of betrayal. There is no dismissal, no closing prayer. Just the awkward silence of, "What do we do now?," which is only a taste of the awkwardness the disciples felt the night the guards took Jesus away.

The most significant day of Holy Week is Good Friday, the day of Christ's crucifixion and death. For us there is the service of the Stations of the Cross during the day, when we join with Christ in his journey from Pilate to the grave. In the evening we gather to give thanks to God for the ultimate sacrifice Jesus made, giving himself up to death that we might know life.

Holy Saturday is the day Jesus' body lies in the tomb, while his spirit descends into hell. We honor this day with a very short, quiet and sweet service of prayer.

Easter Like Christmas, which is a season of twelve days although many Christians only know it as one, Easter is a season of seven weeks, though sadly many Christians only celebrate the single Easter Sunday.

The Easter Season begins with a vigil. Easter Vigil comes on Saturday evening (remember, in the ancient world a day was marked by evening and morning, not by morning and evening). The service has four wonderful parts. First, the kindling of the Paschal flame. The church is dark, and in the center aisle, toward the back, a flame suddenly bursts alive and from this the Paschal candle - the huge candle that remains lit all through the Easter season - is lit. Everyone in the congregation lights their small candle as the Paschal candle passes by them, making its way up to the altar where it will remain until the Day of Pentecost.

The second part of the service consists of several readings from the Old Testament, recounting the story of God's redemption from the fall of Adam, the flood, the Exodus of Moses and the prophecies about the coming Messiah.

Part three of the service is the renewal of our baptismal vows, and the baptism of new believers, when we all confess anew the baptismal covenant.

The final part of the Easter Vigil is the service of Holy Communion when, after forty days of not saying it, we let ring "Alleluia!" The priest shouts out, "Christ has risen from the dead!", and the people respond, "The Lord is risen indeed! Alleluia! Alleluia!"

Easter morning is the most joyous celebration of the entire Christian year. We gather together, having spent forty days identifying with Christ's temptation, having journeyed in a downward spiral from Palm Sunday to Good Friday, and now we join in with the women at the tomb and with the Apostles in celebrating the unbelievable Good News that a dead man got up and walked, having conquered death, hell and the grave, and having opened the way of eternal life to all who believe in him. We sing songs and ring bells and shout shouts, then we have a great feast together to break our Lenten fasts.

Ascension Thursday occurs 40 days after Easter. It is the most overlooked event in the life of Christ, for it is his coronation as King of all creation, when he ascended to the Father and sat down on his heavenly throne, from there to rule the heavens and the earth.

Pentecost Sunday is the end of the Easter Cycle. Fifty days after Jesus rose again, ten days after he ascended to the Father, the promised Holy Spirit fell on 120 believers who were praying together in the Upper Room. This is the Church's birthday! And those who follow the Church year celebrate it every year with a holy fervor.

Ordinary Time   Like the Christmas Cycle, the Easter Cycle is followed by a season of calmness called Ordinary Time. Unlike the Christmas season, the Ordinary Time following Easter lasts for almost half a year. From late spring until four weeks before Christmas, the color is green for growth. Here are no fantastic celebrations, just the day to day growth of believers following Jesus. This season leads back to Advent, when we get to do it all again!

Each season has a special color, fitting hymns and songs, and specific themes. The celebration of the Church year gives definition to our own time, and our own spiritual growth. It declares, year in and year out, that our lives are hidden in Christ's life, and that history is going somewhere - to his Kingdom. Over the span of many years, following the calendar shapes us, and we find ourselves belonging to a great company of saints throughout the ages who have a common faith, a common Lord, a common hope, a common worship, and a common rhythm of life. It is a cast of billions, all singing the same show tune - the Song of the Redeemed.

Chapter Twelve

Getting Into Character:
Sacramental Thinking

When Robert DeNiro was preparing to play the role of Travis Bickle, the mentally disturbed New York taxi driver in Martin Scorsese's 1976 movie *Taxi Driver*, he not only did an in depth study of mental illness, he spent a month working a twelve hour shift as a taxi driver on the streets of New York. Imagine hopping into a taxi for a quick ride over to McSorley's Wonderful Saloon and DeNiro being behind the wheel!

When Jesse Hibbs directed the 1955 movie *To Hell And Back*, the true-life story of Audie Murphy, the Texas farm boy who became the most decorated U.S. soldier in World War II, he convinced Murphy himself to take the lead role. At first, Murphy refused, not wanting to seem self-important, and suggested the role go Tony Curtis. When he finally agreed to play himself, Audie Murphy was able to get into character by simply being the character he was.

As actors in the theater of worship, we too *are playing ourselves*, but it is important for us to get into character before we step onto the stage of God's presence and deliver our lines. Saint Paul admonishes us to present our bodies as living sacrifices to the Lord (Romans 12.1), but we can't truly present our bodies until we present our souls - our minds - our way of thinking.

How Christians Think

Bring up as a topic of conversation among believing friends the idea of having a Christian mindset, and most discussions will turn immediately to two things: ethics and doctrine. At first thought, people assume a Christian mindset means being convinced in mind and heart that there is a biblical code of right and wrong, and that there are biblical truths to be embraced. But let's go deeper than that. Let's take a close look, not at *what* Christians ought to think, but *how* Christians ought to think. And let's call it *sacramental thinking.*

To speak of sacraments is to automatically move beyond the realm of logic and comprehension, and to step into the realm of faith, because the very term sacrament means *mystery.* A sacrament has been classically defined as "an outward and visible sign of an inward and spiritual grace." *The Thirty Nine Articles* state that these sacraments are "not only badges or tokens of Christian men's profession, but rather they be certain sure witnesses, and effectual signs of grace, and God's good will towards us, by the which he doth work invisibly in us, and does not only quicken, but also strengthen and confirm our faith in him."[43]

Unlike sermons and Bible study, which focuses on renewing the mind, sacraments are seen as a mystical participation in the life of Christ himself. When Saint Paul asked the Christians in Corinth, "Is not the cup of thanksgiving a *participation* [*koinonia*] in the blood of Christ? And is not the bread that we break a *participation* in the body of Christ?" (1 Corinthians 10.16ff), he is teaching them that the sacraments are not mere symbols, but are

---

[43] Article 25

instruments of mercy which actually, truly, really do - by the celebration and use of them - graft us into Christ himself, and Christ into us. The sacraments are among "these things" which Saint Peter describes as having *spiritual power* to strengthen our walk with God: "*Through these* he has given us his very great and precious promises, so that *through them* you may *participate* in the divine nature, and escape the corruption in the world caused by evil desires" (2 Peter 1.4).

Unfortunately, many modern Christians have lost the element of mystery in their lives. We live in a materialist age, and our culture teaches us from childhood that the only *real* things are things we can study, dissect and rationally comprehend. If we can't figure it out, we can't embrace it. The ancient Church, with a completely opposite frame of mind, believed in *faith seeking understanding*. I may not be able to comprehend everything God is doing, but I will embrace it in faith, and will seek to understand it as I come to know it experientially.

Symbolic Thinking

One derivative of the materialist mindset which has clung to some Christians like a leech is literalist reading. Now, don't get me wrong, I'm all for reading the Bible literally when the genre in which it is written happens to be literal - like the *history* in the Gospels - but to approach the Psalms literally means God has wings, and to approach Revelation literally means there is a seven-headed dragon lurking out there somewhere, and to approach Genesis literally means the whole fall of humanity was about a single apple (or banana, or kumquat, or whatever the fruit was which Adam and Eve ate). Before anyone sends me hate mail, please understand - I'm *not* saying Adam didn't crunch down on a juicy Gala or Fuji or Granny Smith (did you know there are over 700 varieties of apples in the world - but I digress), but I *am* saying that apple flesh wasn't the real issue, and if you don't know how to think symbolically, you miss the whole point. The real issue wasn't fruit, it was obedience to God. The tree became a symbol of obedience or disobedience. The Bible is full of symbols which have a deeper meaning than the mere physical accidents: the Tabernacle, the Temple, the Ark of the Covenant, the bronze serpent that brought healing when gazed upon, the priestly vestments - these things all *meant* something. They were symbols which communicated truth.

And speaking of symbols which communicate truth...

As human beings we communicate *only* through symbols. Allow me to demonstrate: think of a man wearing a blue shirt. Got it? Now, notice what just happened: I created an image in your mind using nothing but symbols. M-a-n, b-l-u-e, s-h-i-r-t. Letters are nothing but symbols; creative patterns of black ink on a white page. I didn't show you the color blue, I simply gave you a symbol of the color blue and you saw it with your mind's eye. Every word we use, whether spoken or written, is nothing more than a symbol. Our spoken words are but sounds made with the movement of air over our vocal cords and the movement of lips and tongue, but put them in the mouth of John F. Kennedy and you can move a nation to reach the moon. This whole book is nothing but a bunch of symbols, trying to communicate some truth to the reader! Yet, words *do* communicate. They can communicate hatred, scorn, love, passion, beauty, truth, lies, betrayal - anything. The big red sign with S T O P printed on it communicates that you had better cease being in motion at the upcoming intersection. The stop sign is a symbol. As are traffic lights, medicine labels, and recipes and web pages. We even have dictionaries, which are books full of symbols communicating to us the meaning of all the symbols we use!

Words are not the only symbols we use to communicate. A firm handshake, a warm embrace, a special dinner, candles, a birthday cake, wedding rings, clothing, hairstyles, beautiful flower gardens, cosmetics, a star spangled banner, the Alamo - these are all symbols. To reiterate, humans communicate *only* with symbols.

And sacraments are symbols.

But sacraments are *more* than symbols. They not only *represent* an unseen reality, they *convey* that reality; they *deliver* that reality; they *effect* that reality. Sacraments are symbols which *contain* what they symbolize.

Sacramental Thinking

To develop a thoroughly biblical and Christian way of sacramental thinking, three layers of foundation need to be established.

First, *God made matter*. He created the physical world and called it good (Genesis 1-3). The physical world - stuff - is just as much a part of God's design and creation as the spiritual world. Heresies old and new try to promote the idea that the physical world is somehow evil and that salvation is achieved by escaping it (this notion has crept into much of popular Christianity, with its wrong assumption that "eternal life" is about escaping the bounds of earth and going to a non-physical realm called heaven; the Bible, rather, anticipates the redemption of the body in the resurrection, and the re-creation and restoration of this physical universe; cf. 1 Corinthians 15, *et al*). Christianity (and Judaism before it) sees the material world as a blessed and good thing, which God himself made and enjoys, and which God calls us to enjoy.

Second, *God joined matter*. In the incarnation, when Jesus Christ was conceived by the Holy Spirit in the womb of the Virgin Mary, and was born as a human being (albeit fully God), God once and for all time and eternally joined himself to his creation. Not only did he become man, the Word became flesh, deity became matter. In Jesus, in order to redeem and restore *all creation*, God invaded the physical world with his very being. It is proper to say, then, that Christ himself is *the* sacrament of God's grace to us.

Third, *God uses matter*. In joining himself to the flesh of the Virgin Mary - her ovum, her egg - he produced a zygote (interesting that this medical term of the single cell of new life is the Greek word meaning *joined*) which was fully God and fully man. After nine months of gestation, that single cell of the union of heaven and earth was born in Bethlehem and given the name Jesus, and from that time forward, God uses the physical to bring spiritual blessings to his people. From that moment forward, physical creation can be infused with spiritual power and significance, not magically, but by the presence of the living God who has forever joined himself to what he has made.

Sacramental Things

With the foundation laid that God created matter, God joined matter and God uses matter - and therefore God hallowed matter - it remains to be said that all things can become sacramental, can become *vehicles* through which his spiritual power flows. The Apostles understood this. Paul blessed handkerchiefs to be instruments of healing, Peter's shadow healed people, and James wrote that priests should anoint with holy oil and bring wholeness (Acts 19.11, 5.15, James 5.14).

But sacraments, and sacramental things, do not occur willy-nilly, nor by man's own design or power. Classically defined, a valid sacrament requires three things:

Proper form: the right persons, words, prayers and structure of the sacramental moment.

Proper matter: the right "stuff" of the sacrament - water, wine, bread, oil, etc. (you don't use Pepsi in the Communion chalice).

Proper intent: the right reason and intention; a sacrament can't just accidentally happen.

The Church recognizes seven particular sacraments and many additional sacramentals.

The two chief sacraments, baptism and the Lord's Supper, are called the Dominical Sacraments because they are clearly established in Scripture by our Lord (about which, more in the next chapters).

The five lesser sacraments (if it be lawful to call a sacrament lesser), or Ecclesial Sacraments, were exhibited in the ministry of

Christ but formally established by the Church. These are confirmation, holy matrimony, ordination, reconciliation (or confession and absolution) and unction (anointing with healing oil).

Sacramentals include various items and actions blessed for sacred use, including holy water, blessed cloths, and the sign of the cross.

Not only things, but persons and places can be set aside as holy unto the Lord, and become, in a sense, sacramental. To begin with, all Christians are sacramental persons; the Church sets aside bishops, priests and deacons as sacramental ministries; buildings and furnishings can be consecrated as holy to the Lord and blessed to serve as vehicles of God's presence and grace.

In short, for Christians, life is sacramental. We do not live a secular life, enjoying spiritual things only every now and then; rather our whole lives are lived in the presence of God. All we are and all we do should be lived and done in the realization that God is at work in and through us. When we live our lives immersed in sacramental thinking, we grow to recognize and appreciate God working in and through his creation to bring us to fulness in him. The sacraments, as those means particularly chosen by Christ and his Church, are the visible peaks in the great mountain range of holy things through which God accomplishes his purpose.[44]

[44] I cannot strongly enough recommend Alexander Schmemann's *For The Life Of The World* as a deep and stirring *tour de force* of the sacraments and sacramental thinking. New York; St. Vladimir's Seminary Press; 1988.

Chapter Thirteen

The Shower Scene:
The Sacrament of Holy Baptism

One of the most famous murder scenes on stage or screen takes place in a shower. Janet Leigh plays the unfortunate Marion Crane who happens to stay in the wrong place at the wrong time - the Bates Hotel - in Alfred Hitchcock's 1960 thriller, *Psycho*. She had stolen $40,000 from the company she worked for, and was hurrying away to rendezvous with her illicit lover when she checked in to a roadside hotel, had a change of heart, and decided to return the money the next morning, after a good night's rest; that is, after a shower and a good night's rest. The three minute murder-by-knife scene, which has no nudity and never shows the knife touching her body, took seven days to shoot and stands out as the iconic moment of Hitchcock's oeuvre.

In discussing the scene with actress Janet Leigh, Hitchcock communicated what it meant:

> Marion had decided to go back to Phoenix, come clean, and take the consequence, so when she stepped into the tub it was as if she were stepping into the baptismal waters. The spray beating down on her was purifying the corruption from her mind, purging the evil from her soul. She was like a virgin again, tranquil, at peace.[45]

Sir Alfred Hitchcock, the master of cinematic suspense and a faithful Roman Catholic, often dealt with Christian themes in his movies, particularly with underlying Christian ethics and consequences. But here he even uses the very element of baptism to portray a changed heart - water.

It is the most abundant substance on the planet; it is the most essential element

---

[45] Leigh, Janet (with Christopher Nickens), *Psycho: Behind The Scenes Of the Classic Thriller*; New York, Harmony Books, 1995, p. 69f.

known to man; without it, we can't live. We begin our lives cocooned in it, and when it breaks we are born. It refreshes us, cleans us, and sustains our lives. How fitting, then, that it become the singular sacramental symbol of being born - *again* - into the Kingdom of God.

A Short History Of Baptism

Baptism wasn't invented by Jesus; it wasn't invented by John the Baptist, it was just named after him (*I'm just joking! Lighten up a little bit*). Baptism actually has its roots in ancient Judaism as part of a ceremony by which Gentiles converted into the Jewish faith by washing away their old nature, their old lives, and their old sins, through a ceremonial bath. Similarly, if a Jew became ceremonially unclean for any reason, he too went through the ablutions in order to be restored to the community.

The New Testament begins with the story of John baptizing not Gentiles, but Jews, into a baptism of repentance in the Jordan River. Part of his message was that the Messiah would soon arrive who would baptize, not just toward repentance, but into the realm and power of the Holy Spirit (cf. Matthew 3.1-12). The first "Christian" baptism, and the one from which all future baptisms would spring, was the baptism of Jesus himself in the Jordan River. When Jesus was baptized the ceremony itself was changed. In a very real way, the waters of baptism did not make Jesus holy, rather Jesus made the waters of baptism holy - and sacramental. His baptism was a prototype of Christian baptism to come, and two significant things happened at his baptism which define the content and character of Christian baptism.

First, the voice of God said, "This is my Son." In Christian baptism we are made sons and daughters of God. God places his public seal of adoption on us and we are officially received into God's immediate family.

Second, the Holy Spirit descended on Christ. In Christian baptism the gift of the Holy Spirit is given to the believer.

From the baptism of Jesus through the end of the New Testament, the act of baptism stands out as *the singular ceremony of initiation* into the family of God. There is no "walking the aisle," no "coming forward to accept Jesus as my Lord and Savior" no "making a decision to follow Christ," no "praying the sinner's prayer." There is baptism. Period. It is so central and so important that the act of conversion and the act of baptism go unquestionably hand in hand - the two are indistinguishable.

Baptism is part of the Great Commission, when Jesus gave the Apostles their marching order, telling them, "Therefore go and make disciples of all nations, *baptizing them* in the name of the Father and of the Son and of the Holy Spirit, and teaching them to obey everything I have commanded you" (Matthew 28.19f). It is central to the conversion of the multitude on the Day of Pentecost when, "those who accepted his message *were baptized*, and about three thousand were added to their number that day" (Acts 2.41). It figures as *the prominent event* throughout the book of Acts, inseparably linked to conversion (2.38ff, 8.12ff, 8.36ff, 9.17ff, 10.44f, 16.13ff, 16.29ff, 19.5ff, 22.14ff - get the point?).

If baptism tends to not hold the same place in the modern Church as it did in the New Testament Church, there is no need to ask who changed. C.S. Lewis wrote, "We all want progress...[but] if you are on the wrong road, progress means doing an about-turn and walking back to the right road; and in that case, the man who turns back soonest is the most progressive man."[46] Some modern churches (and I'm speaking of churches from practically every denomination) need to make some progress concerning baptism.

What Happens In Baptism?

As a pastor and a bishop I am often asked, "What happens to a person in baptism?" I don't dare just quote Scripture, because it gets me into all kinds of trouble. Well, OK, I *do* quote Scripture, but then I tell people who want to argue that I'm the wrong guy to argue with - I'm just passing on the word from Saint Peter!

> And this water [of Noah's flood] symbolizes *baptism that now saves you* also - not the removal of dirt from the body but the pledge of a good conscience toward God. *It saves you* by the resurrection of Jesus Christ, who has gone into heaven and is at God's right hand... (1 Peter 3.21f).

Baptism saves you. Want to argue about it? Take it up with Simon Peter.

---

[46] Lewis, C.S., *Mere Christianity*, New York, MacMillan, 1958, p. 22.

Western Christians are almost never content with the *what*. They always want an answer to the *how*. "Baptism saves me, eh? Well, just *how* does that work?" Seeing that I'm just a johnny-come-lately in this discussion, I'll leave the explanation to the *Thirty Nine Articles*. "Baptism is not only a sign of profession, and mark of difference, whereby Christian men are discerned from others that are not christened, but it is also a sign of regeneration or new-birth, whereby, *as by an instrument*, they that receive baptism rightly are grafted into the Church; the promise of the forgiveness of sins, and of our adoption to be the sons of God by the Holy Ghost, are visibly signed and sealed; faith is confirmed, and grace increased by virtue of prayer unto God."[47]

The Church has always held that baptism is the birth-waters into a new life in Christ. Consider these New Testament texts as evidence of the centrality and importance of the sacrament:

> Acts 22.16: And now what are you waiting for? Get up, be baptized and wash your sins away, calling on his name.

---

[47] Article 27, *italics added*.

Romans 6.3f: Or don't you know that all of us who were baptized into Christ Jesus were baptized into his death? We were therefore buried with him through baptism into death in order that, just as Christ was raised from the dead through the glory of the Father, we too may live a new life.

1 Corinthians 12.13: For we were all baptized by one Spirit into one body - whether Jews or Greeks, slave or free - and we were all given the one Spirit to drink.

Galatians 3.26f: You are all sons of God through faith in Christ Jesus, for all of you who were baptized into Christ have clothed yourselves with Christ.

Ephesians 4.4-6: There is one body and one Spirit - just as you were called to one hope when you were called - one Lord, one faith, one baptism; one God and Father of all, who is over all and through all and in all.

Colossians 2.11-13: In him you were also circumcised, in the putting off of the sinful nature, not with a circumcision done by the hands of men but with the circumcision done by Christ, having been buried with him in baptism and raised with him through your faith in the power of God, who raised him from the dead. When you were dead in your sins and in the uncircumcision of your sinful nature, God made you alive with Christ.

To put it simply, baptism makes you Christian. It is the spiritual equivalent of matrimony. A couple can live together, love one another, and bear children, but until they are covenantally united in matrimony, no one calls them married. Baptism is our covenantal union with Christ - we take his name as our own in the sacrament. We become Christians. We are born again, born from above. We are given his Spirit. We are brought into the Kingdom of our Lord and Savior and made citizens of his realm.

To Whom Does Baptism Belong?

It would take a complete book to line up the arguments for what I'm about to say, and I'm not in the mood for arguing anyway, so I'll just say it, say a few things about it, and if you really want to get into it, I'll recommend a few resources. Ready? Here it is: from the witness of the New Testament and the early Church, baptism is not only for adults, but also for the children of those who believe.

In the New Testament entire households were baptized into the faith, in keeping with the Old Testament understanding that covenant making is more societal than individual. Some people say this is an argument from silence, and that the Scriptures never specifically *say* any babies or young children were in those households. Agreed. I would also suggest it is an argument from silence to say there *weren't* any babies around, and the likelihood of all the households which believed having *no* children in them, is, well, against the odds (cf. Acts 11.14, 16.15, 16.33, 1 Corinthians 1.16). On the Day of Pentecost, Saint Peter proclaimed, "The promise is for you and your children and for all who are far off - for all whom the Lord our God will call" (Acts 2.39).

Speaking of an argument from silence, the New Testament Church was birthed from a Jewish context, which had no qualms whatsoever about the covenant-initiation of babies. The Law *required* baby boys to be circumcised on the eighth day. It was a given that families were, as a unit, within the continuity of the covenant. The remarkable

224

thing would be for the early Church to have *changed* this principle and said nothing about it. The silence nods in the direction of baptizing babies.

Another nod comes from the immediate witness of the post-apostolic church. Infants of covenant families were presented to God in baptism and marked as Christ's own forever. They were raised, not with the option of becoming Christians when they reached the ripe old *age of accountability*, whatever that is, but with the knowledge that they were already Christians who needed to personalize their faith as they grew in wisdom and understanding.[48] The error in adult-only baptism is in thinking that baptism is something we do for God rather than something God does for us.

I leave the final word on the matter to Michael Green:

These passages, introduced artlessly and unselfconciously into the New Testament narrative, often cause some

---

[48] Infant baptism was affirmed by Irenaeus, Hippolytus, Origen, Cyprian, Gregory of Nazianzus, Chrysostom, and Augustine - all early enough to be *before* the canonization of the New Testament! The earliest clear *refusal* of it, on the other hand, is from the Anabaptists of the 16th Century.

embarrassment in Baptist circles. They rather hope that there were no small children in the families concerned! But surely this is to fail to give sufficient weight not only to the practice of infant circumcision and infant proselyte baptism but to the whole solidarity of the family in the ancient world. We have become so infatuated with individualism that we find this hard to appreciate. But in the ancient world, when the head of the family acted, he did so for the whole family. Where he went they went. All through the Bible we see God dealing with families, Abraham and his family, Noah and his family and so forth. Perhaps it is only the head of the family who expresses faith, but the whole family receives the mark of belonging. The Philippian jailer provides us with a good example of this. He asked Paul and Silas, "'What must I do to be saved?' and they said, 'Believe [singular] in the Lord Jesus and you [singular] will be saved, *you and your household'*...And he took them the same hour of the night and washed their wounds, and he was baptized at once *with all his family*...and he rejoiced with all his household that he [singular] had believed in God. (Ac. 16.30ff)"[49]

In the great drama of our redemption, the play in which we give thanks to God in Christ Jesus, baptism is the shower scene - it is when we come in all dirty from the world of sin, wash up, and get ready for dinner.

---

[49] Green, Michael, *Baptism: Its Purpose, Practice and Power*, Downers Grove, IL, InterVarsity Press, 1987., p. 69f.; for additional study on baptism, and particularly infant baptism, cf. Sutton, Ray R., *Signed, Sealed and Delivered: A Study of Holy Baptism*, Houston, Classical Anglican Press, 2001.

Chapter Fourteen

Dinner Theater:
The Sacrament of Holy Communion

When we rounded the magical corner first discovered that late summer night many years before, the Art Cafe had changed. Julian was still there, but no food was to be had. He had closed the cafe to focus on an art project which might well be his life's greatest achievement: a fifty portfolio tribute for the 400th anniversary of Cervantes' *Don Quixote*, composed of handmade paper, calligraphy, pen and ink drawings, and watercolors - all envisioned by Julian, but brought to life by a team of more than a dozen skilled craftsmen and artists. Disappointed that there would be no dinner but intrigued by the project, Victor,

Debbie, Shirley and I sat down at a table and listened to Julian as he shared his dream.

Eight years before, on a summer evening in the year 2000, my son Ken and I were lost in a foreign city, hadn't had dinner, and were famished. The streets on a map of Toledo, Spain look a lot like a bowl of spaghetti, not a straight lane in the whole place and roads crossing over themselves at least a half dozen times. We had explored the ancient town for an entire day, making our way on foot from one magnificent piece of history to the next, but we had no idea where we were when, in search of late night nourishment, we rounded the corner and found with a stroke of serendipity the Art Cafe. Half art gallery, half bistro, we walked into the little four table establishment and had the place to ourselves. Rather than ordering from the menu, we asked the owner/chef - Julian Simon - to bring us what he thought best, and his eyes twinkled at the opportunity. First, he chose a bottle of wine - a vintage from Ribera del Duero, he told us, a region at the time undiscovered by the rest of the world but loved by Spanish wine connoisseurs. Half an hour later he rounded the corner carrying a tray laden with the best of fare - gazpacho according to his mother's recipe, Spanish sausage made in the old style, dishes of vegetables and beef spiced and cooked to perfection - and he stood there with a look of anticipation as we had our first tastes. Heaven exploded on our tongues. "I use only the best ingredients," he said, "and I prepare it in the old tradition." It was the best meal I have ever eaten.

A year later, when I returned with my wife, I was concerned that I had built up the moment in my mind and perhaps overstated the case for Julian and his culinary skills. I was wrong. It was the second best meal I have ever eaten. Later, my son Ken and his wife Megan went back to Toledo for their honeymoon. I called over and arranged dinner with Julian, and he treated them like royalty on their special occasion.

Back in Spain for the first time in seven years, Shirley and I insisted on taking our close friends, restauranteurs Victor and Debbie Leal, to my favorite restaurant on the planet. But when we walked into the Art Cafe Julian informed us that it was no longer a restaurant, and was instead a simple wine bar. With all his energy being spent on the art project, he had no time to maintain the food service. But that same day, enchantment struck again.

Julian said that although he could not offer us food, he did have wine. His wife sat down at the table and Julian disappeared to a back room. When he returned, there was that familiar twinkle in his eyes which had endeared me to him when we first met. He held in his hand a bottle of wine and looked at me as if I should notice something. "What?" I asked, and he said, "This is the same wine I served you when you first came eight years ago. It is the last bottle, and I have been saving it for a special occasion!" We sat for hours, Julian passionately explaining his art project, Victor and him talking about the culinary crafts, everyone enjoying old and new friends. When the time came to leave, I asked what the cost was for the wine. Julian cast a frown my way, as if I had insulted him, and said, "If you drink alone, you pay me. If I drink with you, you are in my home, you are my guests!"

Saying goodbye and walking out the door, I turned and asked, "Julian, I've told my friends all about your food - where else in Toledo can I find that quality of gazpacho?"

"It is impossible!," he exclaimed with his strong Spanish accent. "But you return in three hours and we have gazpacho!"

"No! I didn't mean for you to make gazpacho for us! I was just asking for recommendations of another place."

"OK," he said, "you come back, or you don't come back. Either way, I will have gazpacho!"

Three hours later we returned to a mini-feast of the best gazpacho in the world, and another hour or two of wonderful conversation.

Julian is one of the most passionate people I know; he puts himself wholeheartedly into everything he does, whether it is cooking or entertaining or crafting a great piece of art. When it comes to food, Julian understands that presentation is every bit as important as taste. What separates dinner at the Art Cafe from a great meal in some other restaurant is one simple truth that Julian knows by heart.

Dining is theater.

The difference between a good meal and a great meal is not just about the quality of food; a great meal is theatrical. There is art involved; presentation is important; it isn't just a nourishment for the body, it is a feast for the taste buds and for the eyes; conversation is had, lines are delivered, and *fellowship* happens.

In Christian worship, the most important act in the play is Act Three, The Service Of The Table. Like the movie *Babette's Feast*, the whole drama builds to the dinner. We come as the people of God to give thanks (*Eucharist* is simply the Greek word for *thanksgiving*) to God for all his benefits toward us, chiefly for what he did for us in offering his Son Jesus Christ for the reconciliation of the world to himself, and we share at table with one another and with God.

A Short History of Holy Communion

It could be said (and the early Fathers *did* say) that the Eucharist has its roots in the Tree of Life in the Garden of Eden. But as a table-meal, the Eucharist finds its beginning in the friendship meal of Jewish rabbis and their students. A teacher and his disciples would gather together, follow a traditional ceremony during a meal, and discuss things of spiritual importance. There is some evidence that the standard number for these groups was the teacher and a dozen disciples, honoring Israel and his twelve sons.

Our celebration of Holy Communion has even deeper roots in the Jewish Passover, a ceremonial meal commanded by God as the children of Israel were preparing to be delivered out of slavery in Egypt and brought into freedom in the Promise Land. God ordered Moses to have the people prepare a lamb, eat it standing, and be ready to hurriedly escape the bondage of Pharaoh. They were to eat the flesh of the lamb, and mark their doors with its blood, that the Angel of Lord might *pass over* them and their lives be saved (Exodus 12). Every year this meal was celebrated as an enduring feast, and became the central act of Jewish worship.

When Jesus gathered his twelve disciples for his final meal with them, it was a combination of these two things - the celebration of the Passover meal, and the celebration of the friendship meal. The four Gospels don't all record all the stories about Jesus. Mark and John have nothing about his birth, for example, but all four Gospels recount the story of Jesus establishing the sacrament of Holy Communion (Matthew 26, Mark 4, Luke 22, John 13). Saint Paul also records the story of Christ instituting the Eucharist (1 Corinthians 11.22-26) and shows that already, early in the life of the Church, the celebration of the Lord's Table was central to the Church's worship of God.

Two things should be noticed in Paul's version of the story. First, he says that he "received from the Lord" the tradition of Holy Communion. Somehow, in some context, the resurrected and ascended Christ instructed Paul about this meal (remember, Paul was a persecutor of the Church and converted several years after the resurrection; Acts 9). However this encounter happened, when Paul wrote about it, he used the same words as the Gospels:

> The Lord Jesus, on the night he was betrayed, took bread, and when he had given thanks, he broke it and said, "This is my body, which is for you; do this in remembrance of me." In the same way, after supper he took the cup, saying, "This cup is the new covenant in my blood; do this, whenever you drink it, in remembrance of me" (1 Corinthians 11.22-25).

Then Paul adds, "For whenever you eat this bread and drink this cup, you proclaim the Lord's death until he comes" (v. 26). Far from being a meal to be casually observed whenever the pastor thought it important enough to get around to, this meal was specifically given by Jesus not only to the original disciples, but also to the late-comer Paul, who would bring the Gospel to the Gentiles.

Second, notice the language Paul uses: "for I *received* (*parelabon*) from the Lord what I also *passed on* (*paredoka*)to you" (v. 23). This is not Paul saying, "hey, let me tell you what Jesus told me". He uses two specific technical words for *the transmission of tradition.* Some modern Christians may shy away from observing traditions, opting instead for a looser structure of sudden inspiration, but in this they part ways with Paul and the other Apostles.

Throughout the entire New Testament era, the history of the early Church, and the first sixteen centuries of Christian faith, the celebration of the Holy Eucharist has been *the central act* of Christian worship. Though abused in the medieval era and ignored (or at least sidelined) by much of the modern Protestant church, in our time Christians from all traditions are rediscovering the importance and centrality of the Lord's Supper and returning to its celebration as the core of worship.

What Happens In Communion?

The Thirty Nine Articles state,

> The Supper of the Lord is not only a sign of the love that Christians ought to have among themselves one to another, but rather it is a Sacrament of our Redemption by Christ's death: insomuch that to such as rightly, worthily, and with faith, receive the same, the Bread which we break is a partaking of the Body of Christ; and likewise the Cup of Blessing is a partaking of the Blood of Christ.[50]

The Church, particularly in the West, has gotten bogged down with philosophical technicalities in attempting to explain the *mystery* of what happens at the altar (can a mystery really be explained?). At one end of the debate, Roman Catholics believe in the dogma of *transubstantiation* - that the physical bread and wine change substance and become the physical body and blood of Christ. On the other end of the debate, some Protestants (following Zwingli) insist that *nothing* happens, and we are eating and drinking only bread and wine as a kind of physical symbol

---

[50] Article 28.

devoid of sacramental reality. The bread is nothing but bread. The wine is nothing but wine - or better, grape juice - a novelty introduced into the Church by Methodist minister, Thomas Bramwell *Welch*, his pasteurized juice first marketed as *Dr. Welch's Unfermented Wine* in 1869. It is all mere symbol (which brings to mind the famous line by the female American novelist Flannery O'Connor, who, arguing that if communion were only a picture of Christ's passion, it was a very unconvincing portrayal, said, "If it is only a symbol, then to hell with it.").

The early Church, (and later the Orthodox in the East and the Anglicans in the west) made no attempt to explain *how* the mystery happened, only insisting *that* the mystery happened. The bread becomes the Body of Christ. The wine becomes the Blood of Jesus. Christ is *really* in the sacrament. Thus, the term, *Real Presence*.

Two words in the New Testament are important contributions in embracing the mystery. The first is *participate*. Saint Paul wrote,

> I speak to sensible people; judge for yourselves what I say. Is not the cup of thanksgiving for which we give thanks a

participation in the blood of Christ? And
is not the bread that we break a
participation in the body of Christ? (1
Corinthians 10.15f).

Participation here is *koinonia*, meaning
"fellowship" or "to have communion
with" (hence the term *Communion*). It carries
the idea of partnership, having a share in a
thing. If you own a building with a group of
partners, it doesn't mean that you own the
bathroom and someone else owns the hallway
and someone else owns the office and someone
else owns the storeroom. It means that you all
own the whole building together. If you have
stock in the Welch's Grape Juice company, it
doesn't mean that you own the bottling
machinery and someone else owns the
pasteurizing vats and someone else owns the
labels. You all own the whole company
together.

When we are in Christ we are partners
with him; we have *koinonia* with him and with
one another. When the faithful approach the
Table of the Lord they *share* in - own shares in
- his sacrifice to the Father, and enjoy the
benefits procured by him. Paul insists that the
bread and the wine is a true fellowship with
the Body and Blood of Christ. When we
receive communion, what is ours is his (our

weaknesses, sinfulness, frailty, humanity; our victories, loves, devotion), and what is his is ours (his suffering, crucifixion, death; his resurrection, exaltation, enthronement in heaven, victory over sin and defeat of Satan and death - and yes, his life giving Spirit). *This* is what happens in the Great Thanksgiving we offer to God!

The second important biblical word is *remembrance* or *remember*. Thousands of churches around the world, which embrace the Zwinglian notion of the *real absence* of Christ in the bread and the wine, nevertheless have carved into their Communion tables, "Do this in remembrance of me" (quoting 1 Corinthians 11.24). If they knew what it meant, they might sandblast the words away.

The Greek word is *anamnesis*, and it doesn't mean what most people think it means. It doesn't mean to fondly remember a thing or to mentally recollect a past event. In fact, actualizing that definition is an impossibility for us. If I were to ask you, "Do you remember when Christopher Columbus planted the Spanish flag on a beach in the Bahamas and claimed it for Ferdinand and Isabela?" your answer would certainly be, "No." You may *know about* it, but you don't *remember* it because it happened on October

12, 1492, and you weren't there! Neither do you remember Jesus dying on the cross. You weren't there. You may know about it, meditate on in, believe it, and understand it, but you don't remember it.

But *anamnesis* doesn't mean to recollect an event. It means to "make present the past which can never remain merely past but becomes effective in the present."[51] The word comes over into English in the medical field: *anamnestic reaction*: "a renewed rapid production of an antibody on the second (or subsequent) encounter with the same antigen." I bet that is as clear as mud! So, unless you are nurse or a doctor, let me put it in plain English. An anamnestic reaction goes something like this: you are out enjoying a picnic with your sweetheart and a nasty old red wasp stings the living daylights out of you. Bang! Ouch! Right on the ear. What you didn't know, because you've never been stung by a nasty old red wasp, is that you are deathly allergic to it. You swell up, turn red, your heart beats faster and you have to go to the emergency room for a shot lest you go into anaphylactic shock. Five years later, you are out boating, enjoying a nice summer day with

---

[51] Balz & Schneider, *Exegetical Dictionary of the New Testament*, Grand Rapids, Eerdmans, 1990; Volume I, p. 85.

your sweetheart, and another nasty old red wasp sneaks up and hits you on your thigh. Only this time, something really strange happens: your ear swells up like it has just been stung too. It hasn't of course; it was stung five years ago, but that sting from the past "happens again" and now it is like you have been stung twice. *This*, my friends, is an *anamnestic reaction*.

And *this* is the word Jesus used when he said, "Do this in remembrance - in *anamnesis* - of me."

Every time we come to the Table, we experience a re-presentation of Christ and his sacrifice; we are entering into that once and for all singular offering of Christ to God which happened 2000 years ago on a hill outside Jerusalem, but which transcends time and space and is therefore eternal - we enter into the eternal moment of that singular sacrifice. Each time we celebrate the Eucharist we offer thanks to God for the reconciling death and resurrection of Jesus, and *his death and resurrection become effective for us in the here and now*. The benefit is not contingent on our understanding it or on our emotional condition; it just *is*. We don't try to close our eyes and furrow our brows and *remember* something we weren't there for, we just experience his presence - his Body, his Blood, his sacrifice, his victory - in the act of Holy Communion.

To Whom Does Communion Belong?

There is, in our modern culture, a desire to be inclusive rather than exclusive, and to be egalitarian toward others, and this desire is commendable on many levels. It recognizes that all people are created by God in his image, and that everyone is worthy of respect and dignity. However, like any good quality, it can be misapplied or taken to the extreme. In our desire to include others in our lives, we still maintain boundaries and privacy - in our personal lives, in our families, nations and religion. There is a tendency in some circles to invite any and everyone to the Table of the Lord. But the Church has historically (and rightly) reserved the Lord's Supper for those who have been baptized.

At first this may seem harsh toward people who are drawn to God and may even have repented of their sins but have not yet had the opportunity for baptism. Particularly in churches which have lost the significance of baptism (and have exchanged it for the sinner's prayer, for example) to exclude some from Holy Communion just seems mean-spirited. But the Lord's Table is a covenant meal, a covenant blessing, and people who have never established covenant do not enjoy the benefits of the covenant.

Our age is an age which has forgotten covenant. Our culture thinks nothing of a man and a woman cohabiting and not being married. We wink, or turn a blind eye, to people having a sexual relationship outside the context of a covenant relationship. It is estimated that in the U.S. alone there are more than six million people living together outside of marriage. So with our cultural blinders, it may be difficult to appreciate a religious ceremony that is exclusive.

But, even in our jaded era, we still recognize boundaries. Citizens of a country enjoy certain benefits that non-citizens do not. The doors of our homes are not open to just anyone who wants to come in at any time. We still think it socially embarrassing when someone crashes a party.

The Supper of the Lord is for the People of the Lord, and entrance into the people (like matrimony is entrance into marriage) occurs in the sacrament of baptism. One of the joys of my ministry is celebrating baptism, and then seeing the newly baptized present the bread and the wine at the altar, and then become the first in the congregation to share in the Body and Blood of Christ. It is not unlike a virgin saving herself for her wedding night.

The Christian life is a life full of sacramental moments. Because one day is holy, all days become holy. Because a place is holy, all places become holy; because one special meal is holy, all meals become holy. Because we are actors in the cast of The Great Thanksgiving, our entire lives become a drama of expanding the Kingdom of God until it comes in fullness. And so we act out our lives to the glory of God and all the world is a stage. And we look forward to that final moment - *curtain call* - when the Audience of One, the King of Kings and Lord of Lords, stands up, applauds, and says, *"Bravo! Bravo! Well done!* Well done, thou good and faithful servant...enter thou into the joy of the Lord."

About the Author

Kenneth Myers was born in 1959 in Denison, Texas. The son of a pastor/missionary, he married Shirley McSorley in 1977. They have three children and three grandchildren. He is an Anglican bishop and pastors Christ Church Cathedral in Sherman, Texas.

www.kennethmyers.net

Made in the USA
San Bernardino, CA
11 January 2016